IN PERFORMANCE

IN PERFORMANCE

Contemporary Monologues
for Men and Women
Late Teens – Twenties

JV Mercanti

Published in 2013 by Applause Theatre & Cinema Books
An Imprint of Hal Leonard Corporation
7777 West Bluemound Road
Milwaukee, WI 53213

Trade Book Division Editorial Offices
33 Plymouth St., Montclair, NJ 07042

Permissions can be found on page 183 which constitutes an extension of this copyright page.

Printed in the United States of America

Book design by Mark Lerner

Library of Congress Cataloging-in-Publication data has been applied for.

ISBN 978-1-4803-3157-0

www.applausebooks.com

CONTENTS

WOMEN'S MONOLOGUES   101

PREFACE

One of the best auditions I've ever seen was for Roundabout Theatre Company's 2001 revival of Stephen Sondheim and James Goldman's musical *Follies*. Jim Carnahan, the casting director, and I had called in Judith Ivey for the role of Sally Durant Plummer. If you don't know who Judith Ivey is, please Google her immediately. You have most likely seen her in something on stage, in film, or on television. You might also have seen a play that she's directed. She is a prolific artist. The role of Sally Durant Plummer is fragile and complex. Sally has been married to Buddy for years and years, but all that time she has been pining for the love of Ben Stone, who is (unhappily) married to Sally's former best friend, Phyllis. Sally is going crazy with love and desire that has been burning for over twenty years.

Ms. Ivey was asked to prepare a cut from Sally's famous first-act song "In Buddy's Eyes," an aria through which she tries to convince Ben that she's deliriously happy in her life with Buddy. She was also asked to prepare a short scene. Present in the room for the audition were Stephen Sondheim, the composer and lyricist; Matthew Warchus, the director; Todd Haimes, artistic director; Jim Carnahan, casting director; Paul Ford, the accompanist; a reader; and myself.

Walking into the room as herself, Ms. Ivey conversed with Mr. Warchus and Mr. Sondheim about her career and, very briefly, about the character. She then took a moment with Paul Ford to discuss the music. Following that, she came to the center of the playing space, closed her eyes, took a deep breath, and prepared herself to begin. In that moment of preparation, which truly lasted no longer than a breath, her body changed, her physicality changed, the very air around her seemed to change. She took the character into her body. Ms. Ivey then opened her eyes, nodded at Mr. Ford, and began to sing.

Ms. Ivey executed the song with specificity, a rich but contained emotional connection to the material, a strong objective, carefully thought-out actions, and a deep understanding of this woman and her love. She went directly from the song to the scene, completely off-book (lines memorized), and when she finished—the room was silent. Mr. Sondheim had tears in his eyes. Mr. Warchus didn't have a word of direction to give her. It was not that Ms. Ivey had provided us with a complete performance. No, not at all. She had shown us the possibility of what she could create. She had shown us the potential of her Sally Durant Plummer. Her point of view was clear, consistent, and deeply, deeply affecting.

"Thank you, Judith. That was wonderful," Matthew Warchus finally said.

"I really love Sally," she responded, "But I was wondering if you might also consider me for the role of Phyllis. I've prepared that material as well."

"Of course I would. Would you like a few minutes to go outside and prepare?" he asked.

"No. No, that's all right. I can do it right now," she responded.

And after saying this, Ms. Ivey closed her eyes. She very slowly turned away from us, put her hair up in a tight bun, and turned around to face the room. It took no longer than thirty seconds, but once again her body, her posture, the way she related to the air around her, had changed. The aura of the room shifted with her. Once again, she nodded at Paul Ford at the piano, and she fearlessly launched into the Phyllis Stone material.

It was astonishing. Not a false note was sung or uttered. Ivey had such a deep understanding of the cold facade Phyllis wears in order to cover up her breaking heart. Phyllis is the polar opposite of Sally: cool, controlled, calculating, and hard.

Ms. Ivey thanked us for the opportunity. We thanked her for her work. The room remained still and silent for a while after she left.

Without a doubt, Mr. Warchus knew he must cast her in the show. She landed the role of Sally Durant Plummer.

It was clear that Ms. Ivey did a very thorough study of the text in preparation for this audition. She understood who these characters were; how they thought; why they spoke the way they did, using language in their own specific ways. She understood how they moved, where they held their weight, how they related to the space around them. Most importantly, she understood the characters' objectives (what they wanted) and how to use the other person in the scene to get what she wanted.

You can achieve the same level of performance as Ms. Ivey if you put the requisite amount of work into your monologue, ask yourself the right questions (or the questions I ask you to examine following each of the pieces in this book), and activate your imagination.

Introduction
Approaching the Monologue

Actors are interpretive storytellers. We often forget that.

You take the words the writer has given you and process them through your own unique instrument (your mind, your body, your imagination, and, hopefully, your heart and your soul), and you turn those words into action—into doing. I'm sure you've been taught by this point in your career that acting is doing. As a teacher, acting coach, and director, I am constantly asking the questions "What are you doing?" and "Why are you doing that?"

I'm also always asking the question "What does that mean?"

Most beginning actors think that memorizing the lines is enough. Or that emoting is enough. As I tell my undergraduate students, acting is hard work, and it's more than just memorizing lines and saying them out loud. It takes emotional connection, analytical skill, a relationship to language, and an understanding of human behavior and relationships to turn the written word into honest, believable action. It also takes rehearsal. Rehearsing a monologue is tricky business, because you don't physically have a partner in front of you to work off of, react to, and actually affect. Oftentimes you'll find yourself staring at an empty chair, saying the lines out loud over and over. Hopefully, what follows will help you deepen your rehearsal process and activate your imagination.

You're reading this book because you're looking for an audition piece. It might be for a non-equity or community-theater production, an undergraduate or graduate program, or a professional meeting with an agent or a casting director. It may even be for an EPA.[1] Whatever the case, you're looking for a piece that—I hope—you feel you connect with on some level; that expresses a particular essence of you; that shows off your sense of humor or sense of self; and that, above all, tells a story you want to tell.

Your monologue choice tells the person (or sometimes the numerous people) behind the table something about you. Certainly it lets us know that you can stand in front of an audience, comfortable in your own body, and perform. It tells us you can open your mouth and speak someone else's words with comfort, confidence, and a sense of ease. It lets us know whether or not you have the ability to project or modify your voice depending on the requirements of the space.

More than that, your monologue choice tells us something about who you are as a person. Your monologue can tell us the type of things you respond to emotionally, intellectually, and humorously. After all, we're going under the assumption that you put a lot of time and care in finding a piece that you wanted to perform. You took the time to commit said piece to memory and to heart. You took the time to practice it over and over again,

---

1   EPA stands for Equity Principal Auditions. All productions that produce on a contract with Actors Equity Association are required to have these calls. The casting department for these EPAs can provide scenes from the play they are casting or request monologues.

translating the author's words into your own. You've imbued it with your sense of humor, understanding, compassion, pain, and so on. More than just telling us whether or not you can act—and a monologue is by no means the only arbiter of this—the monologue helps us decide if we like you as a person, if you're someone we want to work with, study with, teach, and hire.

The monologue is, then, a reflection of you. What do you want us to know about you? This is why not every monologue works for every actor. Choose carefully. If it doesn't feel right, it most likely isn't. If you think it's a possibility, commit to the piece, do all of the work you can on it, and then perform it for people whose opinions you trust—not just people who tell you everything you do is wonderful (as nice as it is to have those people around). Ask someone who can be honest and helpfully critical.

Our first impulse is to ask, "Did you like it? How was I?"

Unfortunately, "like" is subjective. I can *not* like something and yet still be affected by it. Instead, ask questions such as the following: "What did you learn about me from that? What do you think it says about who I am? What was the story? Could you tell what my objective was? Who was I? Did I take you on a journey?"

Then take it to a more businesslike level from there: "What am I selling? Does it play to my strengths? What weaknesses are on display in this piece? Does it seem 'type'-appropriate? Did I display a sense of strength as well as vulnerability?"

I will discuss some of these issues further in the pages that follow. However, it's important for an actor of any age to realize that you are selling yourself, and so you need to think like a businessperson. Play to your strengths and overcome your weaknesses.

And if you can't overcome your weaknesses, learn how to cover them up!

So, you're a storyteller, an interpreter, and a businessperson. I told you acting was hard work. Pursue this career with an open heart and a tough skin, because for all the applause you'll receive, you'll also receive a lot of criticism and rejection. You have no control over *why* you did or didn't get cast. You do have control over your performance in the room. Focus on telling the story, a story you connect deeply to, and that's a safe and sure foundation.

Now let's begin.

Why Monologues?

Monologues give us a sense of your skill level and your personality.

As a professional casting director, I can think of only two instances in which I've asked actors to prepare a monologue for an audition. The first was when casting the Broadway production of Andrew Lloyd Webber's musical *The Woman in White*, directed by Trevor Nunn. All the actors coming into the room, whether auditioning for a leading role or a place in the ensemble, were asked to prepare music from the show, a contrasting song of their choice, and a Shakespearean monologue. Mr. Nunn, a Shakespearean expert, used the monologue as a way to get to know the actors, direct them, and gauge their ability to handle language and to play objectives and actions. I received a number of calls from agents, managers, and actors saying that they were uncomfortable with Shakespeare and maybe they shouldn't come in. However, I assured them this was the way Mr. Nunn worked, and he wouldn't be judging the actors' ability to handle the language requirements of Shakespeare but rather their ability to tell a story and take direction.

The second instance was when casting the Broadway revival of *Cyrano de Bergerac*. David Leveaux, the director, asked the men coming in for smaller roles, such as the poets and the soldiers, to prepare a classical monologue. In this instance, casting *was* dependent on the actors' ability to handle classical language. We were also able to assign understudy roles from these auditions because, based on the actors' monologue choice, we had a sense of who they were and of their technical and emotional abilities.

Now, that's two instances of using monologues in a more than fifteen-year career in casting. Truth to tell, I don't like monologue auditions. Although they give me a sense of who you are, they don't tell me if you can really act. I know some great actors who are terrible with monologues and vice versa.

Nonetheless, as a college professor, I've learned that monologues are very important. Actors use them to audition for a program; we use them for season auditions within the department; and most importantly, my graduating seniors are asked to perform their monologues when they meet with agents and managers after their showcases.

Why? For all the reasons I've previously stated: Do you have the ability to speak with confidence and clarity? Do you have the ability to create a two-minute storytelling and emotional arc? Are you comfortable in your body? Can you play an objective? Can you play an action? Are you in control of your emotional life? Are you someone I want to spend time and work with? A monologue lets us know WHO YOU ARE. So it's important that you *know* who you are. And you don't have to be *one* thing, but again, know your strengths.

There appears to be an unwritten rule in schools that urges people away from "storytelling" monologues. In my experience, though, people are at their most active, engaged, and emotionally connected when they are sharing a personal experience with me. In this book you will find storytelling monologues for this very reason. What you must keep in mind in the performing of them is that we tell stories for a reason. Through these stories, the characters are trying to tell us something about themselves. Therefore, you're telling us something about you when you perform it. It's up to you to decide what that is, but make certain you feel emotionally connected to the piece and that you keep it active and engaged with a clear objective.

Now, in the monologues that don't necessarily contain an obvious "story," what do I mean by "storytelling"? I mean you are giving us a brief glimpse into the larger story of that character. You are living out the experience of—bringing to life—a very specific instance in the life of that character. Your plotting of that experience still needs to have a beginning, middle, and end. You must chart your emotional arc for these pieces just as you would if it were a traditional story. Take us on a journey, just the same. Surprise us.

CAUTION: Try not to beat us over the head by living in one extreme emotion for two minutes and simply playing one tactic the entire time. If you do this, we will stop listening and your monologue will become monotonous.

Choosing a Monologue

I hope you've come to this book as a starting point. The best way to choose a monologue is to read plays. Read lots and lots of plays. Read every play you can get your hands on. Watch movies and television shows. Searching for—and preparing—monologues requires lots of work. Also, it's your job.

Why should you do all this work? The reasons are plenty, but let me expound a few of them.

1. Playwrights are the reason we, as theater professionals, exist. It is our job to honor their work while bringing it to life. You will soon find yourself gravitating to a certain writer or writers. You will want to perform their work. You will seek out productions of theirs wherever you are in the country or the world. You will, eventually, want to work with this playwright and help create new work or revive previous work. You will want to interpret and tell their stories. And—if you move to a city like New York, Los Angeles, or Chicago—you will most likely come into contact with them at one point in time and you can speak with them about their work with knowledge and breadth.

    Conversely, there will be writers you find you don't connect with at all. If this is the case, do not use monologues from their work. You need to love the piece on some very basic level. So even if you can't define why you're not a fan, move on. Pick up the play a few months or years later and read it again. Maybe you'll come at it from a different perspective and it will connect with you. It may never.

Finally, many of these playwrights you love and admire get hired to write, produce, and run television shows. Whether in New York or L.A., you will come across a writer who has moved to the film industry for any number of reasons. You will find, I bet, their heart still remains in the theater, and they will love to hear you are a fan of that work.

2. You'll come across monologues that aren't right for you at this point in your life but can be put on the shelf and pulled out again when you're in your late twenties, early thirties, or even sixties. Yes, people in their fifties and sixties still audition, no matter who or where they are. The work, if you're lucky, never ends.

3. When you read these plays and watch TV shows and films, you're researching. You're finding out which actors are getting cast in the parts you want to play. Follow their careers. This is how you begin to track and define your "type." This is how you learn what parts are out there for you.

The actress Saidah Arrika Ekulona (you don't know who she is? Google her. It's your job) spoke to my students last year and said, "Don't worry about so much about your type. Don't obsess about it. Somebody, somewhere is ready to put you in a box, so why should you do it for yourself?" I wholeheartedly agree—and disagree—with her! Here's where I agree: of course you must believe you can do anything, play any part. You need to constantly raise the bar for yourself so that you have goals to achieve. Just because you're the "ingénue" or "the leading man" doesn't mean you can't also find the humor, sexuality, and hunger in those roles. You need to find the complexities and polarities in every role you play. People are complicated, and therefore so are characters.

However, you also need to keep in mind that this is a business. And people in business want to know how you're marketable. So if you have a list of actors who are doing the things you know how to do, playing the parts you know you can play, you are armed with information that's going to help you market yourself. Don't think of defining your type as a "box." It's not. It's a marketing strategy.

It may sound like a cliché, but knowledge is power. And your knowledge of these plays, writers, and fellow actors is your weapon. Put it to use.

4. Films and TV are fair game when searching for material. However, you want to stay away from material that would be considered "iconic." Avoid characters that are firmly ingrained in our popular culture. Shows like *Sex and the City* or *Friends* have great writing, but that writing became more and more tailored for the specific actors playing those roles as the seasons progressed. It is difficult to approach that material without hearing the voices of those actors in our heads. So enjoy those shows, but don't use them, even if your type is a Carrie, a Joey, a Chandler, or a Charlotte.

5. Sometimes you'll find a character that you really like but who doesn't have a stand-alone monologue in the play. You'll be tempted to cut and paste the lines together until you form it into something that seems complete. I caution you away from this. Although some of the pieces in this book have been edited, there has been no major cutting

and rearranging. Any edits to the following monologues consisted mainly of stage directions or brief responses by the other characters in the scene that did not interrupt the flow of thought on the part of the character delivering the monologue. Some of these pieces, such as Lisa Kron's *Well*, are part of longer monologues. There have been no internal cuts or edits within the presented monologues. I find that it destroys the author's intent. You're crafting a piece into something it wasn't meant to be. Look at something else by this writer. Or search for a similar character in another play. Your "type" work will come in handy here. The actor who played this role was also in what other plays? This writer has also written what other plays?

6. Once you've chosen a monologue from this book (or from a play or film), please read the entire work. Then read it again. Then—read it again. Although you will ultimately be performing the piece out of context, you can act it only if you can make sense of the context in which it was written.

Preparing the Monologue

1. Read the entire play.
2. Read the entire play again.
3. Read it one more time.
4. Although you will have been very tempted to do so, do NOT read the monologue out loud yet. You've read the play a few times now, and you're beginning to, consciously or unconsciously, realize the intention of the piece in the whole.

I want you to think about the play as a whole, first, by asking these questions:

Is this a dramatic or a comedic monologue?

This is a tough question. I find that most good monologues walk the line between the two, putting them firmly in the "seriocomic" category. A comedic monologue is not always about landing a joke. A comedic monologue shows that you can handle material that is light and playful while still playing a strong objective. A dramatic monologue tackles more serious issues, events, and emotions. Be careful that your dramatic monologue doesn't dissolve into you screaming and/or crying in the direction of the auditioner. This is NOT a sign that you can act. If you're crying and screaming, then you are most likely not playing toward an objective while using strong actions.

In life, we rarely get what we want when we scream or cry at people. It's no different in acting.

What are some of the major themes of the play?

It is often easiest to define your character's objective by wording it to include the main themes or images in the play.

Themes are the major ideas or topics of the play, together with the writer's point of view on these topics.

What does the title of the play mean?

The author's intention or point of view is often most clearly defined in the title of the play. Thinking about it might also lead you to define the main theme of the work, as just discussed.

Who is the main character in the play?

Whose story is it? What is their journey? If you're performing a monologue of the main character, how does the piece affect their progression? If you're performing a piece from a supporting character, how does it assist or impede the main character's journey?

The main character is the person who takes the biggest journey over the course of the play. Your monologue is one of the following: (1) The person on that journey; (2) a person helping the main character on that journey; (3) a person creating an obstacle to the main character achieving their goal.

What is your objective?

This question is twofold, because I'm asking you to define your objective for both the play and the monologue. You need to define what this character wants throughout the entire play, from the moment he or she steps onto the stage. Then you need to define how this two-minute (or so) piece fits into the whole.

An objective is a SIMPLE, ACTIVE, POSITIVE statement that defines the journey your character is on.

It is in defining an objective that most young actors tend to hinder their performance. You never want to define your objective in the following ways: (1) I want "to BE something," or (2) I want "to FEEL something." These are passive, inactive statements in which you will not make any forward progression. Emotion does play a role in acting, but not when it comes to defining an objective.

Instead I want you to define it in very vivid, active words that inspire you and spark your imagination. This is where your knowledge of the entire play and the character you are creating comes into action.

Begin by thinking in very primal terms. Objectives should hold life-or-death stakes. Companionship, shelter, protection, nourishment, sex, fight, flight.

"I want to hold my family together" is a very strong objective.

"I want to make someone love me" is another.

However, I challenge you to take it a step further. In a play like *Jailbait* by Deirdre O'Connor, which is represented later in this book, you might say something like "I want to break out of the cage that confines me" so that you use the language of the play in order to define your objective. Or if you're working on Kirsten Greenidge's *Milk Like Sugar*, you might say, "I want to taste the sweetest, most expensive milk I can find." The more vividly you can paint the objective, especially by using words and images from the play itself, the better.

Play your objective with the belief that you're going to WIN! Play positive choices.

What are the beats and actions?

A *beat* is a transition: a change in thought, action, subject, or tactic.

Actions are active verbs that define what you are doing in any particular moment. Meaning, you attach an active verb to *every line of text*: to sway, to punish, to defend, to challenge, and so on.

Actions become your roadmap, your markers. If you're a musician, think of them as musical notes. The note is written there, but it's up to you to color it, make it your own, and endow it with meaning. Engage your own unique point of view to make it personal. However, every new action does not necessarily mean you've come to a beat change. Feel it out instinctively.

When it feels like there is a shift, there most likely is. That is your beat. Are you accomplishing what you want? Are you winning? If not, it's time to shift your tactic.

Have you been playing the same tactic over and over and not achieved your goal? It's time to shift your tactic.

You cannot consciously play these objectives, beats, actions, and tactics, but you must rehearse with them in mind so that you can internalize them. Once they've become internalized, they will play themselves. It's a form of muscle memory.

Check in with your (imaginary) scene partner. Make sure your actions are landing.

Playing actions helps in two areas: it helps you do more than play the "mood" of the piece. Mood is established in the arc of the storytelling, not in the way you say the lines. Mood is also established in how you're relating to the other person: are you winning, or losing? Secondly, playing actions will help you not play the end of the monologue at the beginning. If the monologue ends in death, you don't want us to know that when you start. Take us there without letting us know we're going to get there.

When I was working as the assistant director of Martin Mc-Donagh's Broadway production of *A Behanding in Spokane,* John Crowley, the director, would sit at the table with the actors every afternoon after lunch and make them assign actions to every line of text. We did this for weeks. It is oftentimes very frustrating, but it lets you know where you're going. It forces you into specificity.

And if any particular action doesn't seem to work for you, throw it out and try another! That is why actors rehearse.

Right now you're asking yourself why you need to do all of this work. Let's go back to the words that opened this book: Actors are storytellers, and the best stories are those told with specificity. Think of this monologue as a smaller story inside a larger one. You need to understand the larger story the playwright is telling in order to tell this shorter story. You need to know the details in order to bring them to life.

The greater your understanding of the piece as a whole, the better your ability to interpret it.

Remember, people rarely expect to speak in monologue form. Have an expectation of how you think your (unseen) partner may react. This is part of a conversation, and your partner is letting you speak for quite a bit of time, or you are not letting them get a word in. Don't approach it as a monologue; approach it as dialogue. Expect your scene partner to cut you off. Your expectation is key to why you go on for some two minutes. Pay attention to and play with your partner. Oftentimes this expectation of interruption will help you bring a sense of urgency to the piece.

Inevitably, you will be performing these monologues for someone who knows the play. You want your acting of the monologue to be consistent with the tone, theme, and style of the play as well as the character's objective within it. You can't take a monologue from *Macbeth*, for example, and mine it for high comic potential. You'll look foolish, and the casting director will assume you don't know what you're doing.

Who is your character?

Once you've answered all of the above questions, it's time to start putting this person into your body.

1. What do they look like?
2. How do they dress?
3. How do they stand?
4. Where is their center of gravity?
5. How do they take up space?
6. What's their posture?
7. Where does their voice sit (i.e., head, throat, chest, diaphragm, etc.)?
8. Where do they hold tension?
9. How do they walk, sit, and stand?

It's up to you to find this person in your body, experiment with them. Holding on to what you know about them from the script, and your very strong objective, you'll be able to find physicality for them through your knowledge of them.

Whom is the character talking to?

These are monologues, but you need to have a very specific picture of WHOM you are talking to, because it plays directly into WHY you are talking (your objective). Some of these monologues are to a specific person, or persons; some were written as audience address. You still need to decide to whom, specifically, it is directed and have a clear image of that person.

Place that person somewhere in the room with you. You should never perform your monologue directly to the person for whom you are auditioning unless they ask. You can place them, in your imagination, to the left or the right and a little in front of that person. You can place them behind that person and a little above their head. You can place them closer to you, to your immediate left, right, or center. However, make sure that they're not so close that you are forced to look down while you deliver your monologue. We need to see your face.

Now that you've placed your "acting partner" somewhere, you need to imagine what it is they look like.

1. What are they wearing?
2. Are they sitting, or standing?
3. What is your relationship to them?
4. What do you need from them (this ties in to your objective)?
5. How is delivering this monologue bringing you closer to achieving your goal?
6. By the end of the monologue, did you win? Did you get what you wanted? Are you closer or further away from achieving you goal?

What's so urgent?

Younger actors often lack a sense of urgency. Remember, your character is dealing with life-and-death stakes! Remember that acting occurs *on* the lines, not in between them. Try to express what you're feeling by coloring a word or a phrase with your point of view while maintaining the flow of the line. Act ON the line not AROUND it. Tie your thoughts together without breaking the line apart in pieces in an attempt to highlight certain words. The line is your thought and your action: present it completely. Try not to add moments, beats, unexpressed thoughts, and feelings in between the lines. It's not necessary. Use what the playwright has given you.

Emotional Connection

Up until now I have hardly mentioned feelings, emotions, or emoting. You must, of course, have a strong emotional connection to the monologue you choose. Your connection may grow or dissipate when you complete the work outlined above. Sometimes the more you discover about a play, or a character, the further it feels from your initial response. If this is the case, and you can't reclaim that initial spark, then move on to something else. You can always find another piece.

Conversely, your initial response to the monologue might be only so-so until you do more work on it, finding yourself truly enlivened and engaged by it. In that case, take it and run.

Acting is not about emoting. Young actors tend to find pieces with very high emotional stakes that often require crying or screaming in order to accomplish the storytelling. Please shy away from these. We want to see that you are connected to the material and that you know how to control your emotional life. We do not want to have your emotions unleashed upon us in a flood that you cannot contain. Therefore, a monologue that occurs at the climax of a play is probably best left performed in the context of the show.

Stay true to yourself and, in doing the work just outlined, you will stay true to the piece.

Finally, it's time for you to put all of the pieces together. You have all the elements of the story, and now you need to get from point A, to point B, to point C. This takes a long rehearsal process.

It means experimenting with all of these elements. If something does not work, throw it away and try something else. If something seems to maybe, kind of work, hold on to it and experiment inside of that. Try doing the entire piece in a whisper and see what you learn. Try doing it at the top of your voice in a public place and see what you discover. Experiment and take risks with how you rehearse it and you might find something you never knew was there.

I strongly urge you NOT to practice these monologues in front of a mirror. It will only make you feel self-conscious, and you will put your focus and energy into how you look while you do it rather than into what you are DOING. Instead, practice it in front of friends and family. Practice achieving your objective on them. Practice your actions on them.

You have created a roadmap, but that doesn't mean you can't take side trips. Your objective is in mind; now try a roundabout way of getting there. Remember, these are called "plays," and you should, in fact, play. Have fun.

In Performance

You are ready to perform the monologue in public. Here are a few quick tips for the audition room:

1. Arrive early. At least fifteen minutes before your appointment time. You need this time to unclutter your mind, focus yourself, and relax.

2. When your name is called, close your eyes and take a deep breath in and out. Find your center.

3. Take as few of your personal items into the room as necessary. Try not to bring in your jacket, your bag, your purse,

your gym clothes, and so on. Gentlemen, please take phones, keys, and loose change out of your front pockets; do not interrupt the natural line of your body.

4. Say a friendly "Hello" to the person or persons in the room, even if they seem engaged in another activity. Very often, we are writing notes about whoever just left the room, but we will try to make contact and greet you, the next person entering the room, especially to see if you look like your headshot.

5. Look like your headshot.

6. Do not advance on the table, introduce yourself, and attempt to shake hands. Keep a friendly, professional distance unless the person behind the table makes a move otherwise. We sometimes see a hundred people in one day; we can't shake everyone's hand.

7. Do not apologize for what you're about to do or explain that you:
   a. Are sick.
   b. Have just been sick.
   c. Feel as if you're getting sick.

8. Find a comfortable space to stand, or ask for a chair if you're using one. There will almost always be a chair available for you. It makes no difference to us whether you stand or sit, but it sometimes makes a difference to your monologue.

9. Once you're in position, please introduce yourself and let us know the title of the play from which the monologue comes.

10. Take a moment before you begin. Close your eyes or turn away from us. Center yourself. Runners don't hit the track

and begin running. They take their position, they focus themselves, they wait for the gun, and then they go. In this situation, you are in charge of the gun. The room is yours when you walk in. As you arrived some fifteen minutes before entering the room, this shouldn't take more than a second or two. Please no slumping in place, no shaking out your arms and legs, no vocalizing. All of this should be done at home or outside the room. The moment before is simply to focus.

11. Act! Have fun. We want you to be good. We want to welcome you into our program, our school, our cast. Worry less about getting it "right" and concentrate on telling us a story.

11a. Sometimes you start off on the wrong foot. That's okay. You can stop and ask if you can start again. Take a breath. Focus. Start again. If it doesn't happen the second time, you should kindly apologize and leave the room. You're not prepared. You've not done enough work on the piece, or you're letting your nerves get the better of you. There are no tried-and-true tricks for beating this. Comfort and familiarity with the material, combined with a desire to tell the story, are your best bets!

12. Keep it to two minutes. All of the monologues in this book fulfill that requirement, and some are shorter. You do not need to use the entire two minutes. We can very often tell if we're interested in someone within the first thirty seconds to a minute.

13. When you've finished, take a beat and end the piece. Give us a cue that your performance is over and you're no longer the character. Again, be careful of judging your work

while in the room. I've seen many actors want to apologize or make a face that says, "Well, that didn't go the way I had planned it." Whether it was your best work or your worst work, don't let us know.

14. There's a fine line between lingering and rushing out of the room. Sometimes we may ask you a question or two in an effort to get to know you better. Stay focused and centered until we say, "Thank you."

15. Your résumé should be a reflection of your work. Please don't lie on it in any way, shape, or form! Don't say you've worked with people or on productions that you never have! If you were in the ensemble, don't say you were the lead! We've all been in the ensemble. It's okay.

16. Enjoy telling the story!

In this book I'm providing you with a summary of the play, a brief character description, and a list of questions you should ask yourself when approaching the material. However, I urge you to seek out the play and read it in its entirety so that you can have a greater understanding of the character, the situations, and the events.

Most importantly, when performing any of these pieces, play a strong, simple, vivid objective; maintain a deep emotional connection to the material; act on the line; have a sense of urgency; and know why, and to whom, you're speaking.

Men's Monologues

The Drunken City
Adam Bock

BOB

I got that ring in Mexico. After my last boyfriend When he broke up with me I bought it for myself. I was in Mexico. And he wasn't in love with me anymore Because he got lost in the relationship Because I must have done something. That's the reason. I'm sick of love. It's too hard.

I meet a guy and at first he's himself with me. He kisses me because he wants to and it's fun He's pushing himself all up against me and I get to push back and it's fun He's trying his tricks he's got all his tricks going and he's juggling and joking and that makes me laugh and it's fun

and then

all of a sudden He falls in love and suddenly it's all "let's put candles in the bathroom" and "I think I'm in love" and

(*He makes googoo eyes.*)

And then he forgets who he is. And he gets mad at me for that. And says it's because I'm too hard on him. So I'm "forget about it."

Enough's enough. I'm done with it. And it's ok. It's good. I'm ok. I work hard. I like working. I love my job. That's what I love.

Analysis: *The Drunken City*

Type: Seriocomic
Synopsis

People meet. They fall in love. They get engaged. They get married. They live happily ever after. Or that's how it's supposed to happen. Adam Bock's play *The Drunken City* dissects the heart of relationships in that very tenuous time between engagement and marriage, exploring the many false justifications people create for such a sacred event.

In the first scene, three young women, all best friends, descend upon an unnamed city to celebrate the fact that they've (all three of them) recently become engaged. Marnie is engaged to Gary. Melissa is engaged to Jason. Linda is engaged to Jack. Marnie and Melissa work together at the Sunshine Bakery. Linda comes in and eats the muffins. All three are over the moon with excitement.

Fast-forward three weeks, the ladies are back in the city for Marnie's bachelorette party. Melissa has discovered that Jason was cheating on her, and she's no longer engaged. They have spent the day shopping for bridesmaids' dresses. Suddenly a drunken Marnie finds herself kissing a man, Frank, on the street. This event (and numerous others over the course of the evening) causes the entire world to, literally, tilt. Every time the world tilts, the characters slide from one side of the stage to the other or, sometimes, even on and off stage.

This drunken night causes Marnie to seriously question her relationship with Gary and her motivations for marrying him. Frank, recently out of his own long-term relationship, listens to Marnie in a way that no one else ever has. Melissa, still reeling over her breakup with Jason, refuses to let Marnie sabotage her relationship with Gary. She calls in their boss, Bob, to come and help talk some sense into Marnie. Bob has his own relationship problems, though, and doesn't really have the skills necessary to help anyone. He finds himself falling unexpectedly for Frank's best friend, Eddie.

Bock's play is far from a condemnation of marriage or traditional relationships. He is, however, forcing the audience to approach these commitments with an awareness of their partners as well as of themselves. All of these characters reach a certain level of understanding because of the events of one drunken night.

Character Description
Bob, mid-20s

Owner of the Sunshine Bakery. Melissa calls him in to the city to help defuse the budding relationship between Marnie and Frank. Bob is hurt that he wasn't invited to be part of the bachelorette party, but he comes in to help anyway.

Bob has had a bunch of boyfriends and none of them have worked out. Though single at the moment, Bob keeps two pillows on his bed because he's "hopeful." Bob spends so much time with the girls because he's knows little about how love actually works and he's hoping to learn something from them. Marnie suggests that, perhaps, he needs to learn how to love "easier." He finds the potential to do that in Eddie.

Given Circumstances
Who are they? Bob and Eddie have just met. Their friends have run off to make out and they're trying to find them.

Where are they? A city street at night.

When does this take place? Contemporary.

Why are they there? Bob has been called in to help. Eddie and Frank were out picking up women.

What is the pre-beat? Eddie has noticed Bob's ring and Bob, Eddie's. They exchange them to take a closer look.

Questions

1. How many relationships has Bob been in?
2. How does he meet these men?
3. How do the relationships end?
4. What is it about Eddie that allows Bob to share this?
5. What does the ring look like?
6. What does Eddie's ring look like?
7. What does Eddie look like?
8. What does Bob like about baking?
9. Why is Bob jealous that the girls didn't invite him to the bachelorette party?
10. How does Bob feel being the only sober person surrounded by drunks?
11. How far did he have to travel from home to get to the city?
12. Does Bob think Marnie should marry Gary?
13. How is Bob hard on the guys he dates?
14. Does Bob wish he could get married?
15. Bock's language lacks proper punctuation at times; how does this define Bob?

Mercy
Laura Cahill

STU

I've already written one novel.

Yeah. I submitted it to Random House.

Well, I knew this guy who I went all the way through school with in Pennsylvania. He was a real dork actually, I mean you never would in a million years expect this guy to have even made anything of himself, you know, he just didn't "have" it. I don't know how the hell he became so important, but he's an editor anyway at Random House. So I called him up and he was like "Oh great," and we had lunch and he invited me and a bunch of other guys from our group in high school to a big party once and I saw Jay McInerney there. So, um, anyway, I told him I'm writing this novel and he said, "Oh, sure, just send it to me," and so I did and yesterday I got this letter back. And it was from an assistant. That asshole didn't even give me enough respect to take my manuscript and put it on top of his own desk and read it and let me know what he thought. I don't even know who this Bozo is who read it or how qualified they even were to give me their opinion.

Well, whatever, it doesn't really matter. I'm trying short stories now. I'm interested in the form. It challenges me.

So I'm working on pursuing it full time.

Yeah. I'll always be a doctor.

Analysis: *Mercy*

Type: Seriocomic
Synopsis

In Laura Cahill's funny, touching, and unsettling play, everyone is talking but no one seems to be listening. At one point the
character Sarah reads aloud from her journal: "General feeling of
emptiness and loss. Sort of—almost. I have a feeling of almost."

This feeling of "almost" pervades the entire play. Each of
the four characters seems to be (or wants to be) on the brink
of something, something indefinable, yet not a single one of
them can commit to achieving it. If these young people could
muster up the courage to actually *do* something, make a decision, take a step, put their feelings on the line, then life would
perhaps take a turn in their favor. They are, however, frozen.
They cannot find a "flow" in life because they are unable to
see past themselves.

Isobel, the main character, is heartbroken over her recent
breakup with Stu. Stu is a doctor who dreams of being a writer.
Sarah, Isobel's best friend, says she wants to cheer Isobel up, but
she spends most of her time aggressively pursuing Bo. Bo has
recently declared himself a singer/songwriter after a failed attempt at acting.

These four people are unable to make any kind of meaningful
connection with each other.

At the end of the play, Isobel declares her love for Stu. His response to this outpouring of emotion is, "I don't know how to respond to that." Therein lies the tension of the play: no one knows how to respond to each other's needs. Isobel, more than any of them at the moment, needs some mercy in her life, but no one around her can grant it.

Character Description
Stu, mid-20s

Stu's specialty is, ironically, internal medicine. I say "ironically" because although he may have a great knowledge of the body's biology, he hasn't an inkling about its psychological or emotional needs.

Isobel states that one of the reasons their relationship ended was Stu's inability to relate to her feelings. He would say things like, "I have to laugh because you can't possibly feel that way." How does he know what she's feeling?

Stu dreams of becoming a professional writer. He has actually written something. He has asked someone to read it. He has tried to take a step out of his comfort zone. Unfortunately, upon this first rejection, he gives up on that work and decides to change forms entirely, switching from novels to short stories. This action immediately dismisses all the work he has accomplished.

At dinner, when the group is choosing music, Stu requests music without words since he doesn't listen to them because he never learned to sing. He is a doctor who doesn't listen to words or understand feelings! His realization at the end of this monologue that he'll always be a doctor must be huge and life-altering.

Given Circumstances

Who are they? Isobel and Sarah are best friends. Stu and Bo are friendly. As a group they are strangers and relate to each other as such.

Where are they? Sarah's Upper West Side apartment.

When does this take place? Contemporary.

Why are they there? A dinner party.

What is the pre-beat? Bo has finally performed for the group the song he wrote, impressing the two women.

Questions

1. Why did Stu and Isobel break up?
2. How long had they been together?
3. How did they meet?
4. What did Stu like about Isobel?
5. How did Isobel not measure up to Stu's standards?
6. What does "internal medicine" mean?
7. What is the demeanor of a doctor?
8. Does Stu like any part of being a doctor?
9. Why does Stu want to be a writer?
10. What is Stu's novel about?
11. What are his short stories about?
12. When does he make the time to write?
13. There's a huge shift between the short-story section and "I'll always be a doctor." What happens there?
14. Why doesn't Stu understand how Isobel, or others, feels?
15. Why did Stu come to this dinner party, knowing Isobel will be there?

From Up Here
Liz Flahive

CHARLIE

You're a sophomore, right? Kenny Barrett's sister? (*She nods. Beat.*) Charlie. (*Beat.*) Senior. (*Beat.*) You going to the dance on Friday?

People say you fucked two guys at Kristi Shinnick's party last weekend? Did you know people are saying that?

David Blitzstein said the minute he put it in you, you started crying. Did he hurt you?

Because it's only supposed to hurt the first time. I mean, it's not like I know, but I do because I talk to girls and they tell me stuff like, well not exactly what happens. I don't press for details because it's private — it's not that but I have close girl friends, not girlfriends but we talk about sex. Not just about sex but it's well, it's topical. Mostly sex is just topical, it's not paramount, not yet, anyway, because it's all just started or not started or not that good but, I guess it's safe to assume it will become a serious variable. At some point. But sex is not the most important thing and I think a lot of people feel compelled to decide what the most important thing is, especially right now. I don't understand it, ordering the importance of everything. Like how everyone's all obsessed with class rank, who's number 20, who's right up next to you at 19. And fine, I think it's good to know where you stand and but it's like everyone is so hung up on trying to get the least important things to matter the most. Whatever. But, see, I love walking around, knowing what I want. That's actually useful. To think about something, and really want it. And then you see it and knowing it actually exists is . . . It's this feeling like I'm looking at everything through one of those cardboard tubes, the ones that hold paper towels and everything's all . . . (*makes a circle with both his hands and extends one out like a handheld telescope*) And I know what I want is to stand next to you and talk to you. Here I am. Doing exactly what I want. So this. Yeah. This is such a great day. Already. And it's pretty early. (*Beat.*) Hey. (*Beat.*) Bus.

Analysis: *From Up Here*

Type: Seriocomic
Synopsis

Kenny Barrett, a high school senior, has threatened his high school with an act of unspecified violence. The act was unsuccessful, but the resulting aftershocks are deep and lasting. He has been allowed back into school, but under the provision that he be constantly supervised, on campus and at home. The potential of the event has left everyone in Kenny's family feeling unsettled. This unsettled feeling—mixed with a sharp dose of violence—causes the play to practically vibrate.

Grace, Kenny's mother, and Daniel, her new, much younger husband, are on uncertain footing. Daniel is keen on starting a new family, bringing a new child into their lives. Grace feels she can't handle the children she has now. The household is thrown into further chaos by the unexpected arrival of Caroline, Grace's unpredictable younger sister. Kenny feels an affinity for Caroline that he does not share with his mother. This relationship further pushes Grace off balance.

Kenny's younger sister, Lauren, is confused by the actions of her brother. She's trying desperately to understand why he was planning the violence; why he would hurt himself and others; and why he would leave her alone. She is surprised and confused by the sudden attention of Charlie, an upperclassman. Charlie doesn't look at her strangely, or as the sister of a freak. He simply sees *her*.

From Up Here is about holding on to each other even when the world seems to be falling apart around you.

Character Description
Charlie, 17

A high school senior, he's a singer/songwriter who plays both the guitar and harmonica. This monologue is the first interaction he has with Lauren. Later in the play, he writes a song for her and plays it in the school parking lot. He even gets Kenny to join in on the chorus. He is a romantic and has strong feelings for Lauren. He says to her, "When I think about you I can't breathe and I look at you and I'm not sure you're real."

He parks his car and takes the bus just to be near Lauren. Slowly but surely he begins to win her over. She agrees to go to the school dance with her. On the night of the dance he even brings Kenny a CD to make him feel included.

Charlie is thoughtful, brave, and careful. He respects Lauren and doesn't want to rush the sexual components of their relationship until they're both ready for it. He's happy just to be with her and take things slowly.

Given Circumstances

Who are they? Charlie and Lauren go to the same high school but are in different classes. Kate, another classmate, is standing nearby.
Where are they? A bus stop.
When does this take place? Contemporary.
Why are they there? It's morning and they're on their way to school.
What is the pre-beat? Charlie has parked his car and come to stand at the bus stop.

Questions

1. What does Charlie find attractive about Lauren?
2. What does she look like?
3. How does he feel about her brother Kenny?
4. What does he want from Lauren?
5. Does Charlie worry about what other people will think if he succeeds in dating her?
6. How long has he had his eye on her?
7. Why is he approaching her today, finally?
8. How does his use of language define who he is?
9. What does he hope her reaction will be?
10. How big is their school — that is, how many students in each grade?

11. What kind of feeling does Charlie get from playing and writing music?
12. What kind of feeling does he get from looking at Lauren?
13. What kind of student is Charlie?
14. What are his plans after graduation?
15. How does the fact that Kate is standing nearby inform the delivery of this monologue?

Milk Like Sugar
Kirsten Greenidge

MALIK

HEY. You tryin' a hit it pretty quick, yo. You diggin' at me like I'm some sort of grab bag at a kiddie party, right? You don't even ask me do I got protection or nothin'. I ain't thinking about being somebody's daddy.

I don't like those people up in that plane laughing at me. Cause the way I imagine it, they see me from my window, Annie. They see into my window, they see the paint curling off the walls, they see my mom ain't done the washing in weeks, they see there ain't more than two packages macaroni and cheese in the cupboard. They see that and they mouths crimp up into smiles and I wanna crush those smiles. 'Cause all they see is some bone head baby daddy don't know enough to use a rubber and end up stuck — paint curling, milk like sugar on the shelf. I do this like you want I be stuck forever with them laughing at me. Make my skin burn. You think about that? People like them folks in that plane up there? Laughing down at you like that? You and Talisha and all y'all can rot in this place but I won't. Thought you wouldn't want to either.

Analysis: *Milk Like Sugar*

Type: Dramatic
Synopsis

It is Annie Desmond's sixteenth birthday. She is celebrating with her best friends, Margie and Talisha, by going to a tattoo parlor. Annie initially wants a ladybug. Under pressure from Talisha, who says that is silly and childish, she decides instead on a small red flame on her hip. This pull between childhood and maturity is the main theme of the play. The three girls also form a pact on this day, sparked by Margie's pregnancy, to have babies at the same time.

Milk Like Sugar paints a startlingly candid take on the adolescence of African American inner-city youth in contemporary America. Annie's home life is difficult. Her undereducated mother, Myrna, is a cleaning woman who dreams of being a writer. Her father is mostly absent. Her friends care more about which boy has the best new cell phone and what kind of designer baby gear they'll get than anything else. Talisha is in a relationship with a much older man who abuses her. Margie's man is mostly undefined. For these girls, the joy of having a baby comes from the search for unconditional love. They feel unloved, unwanted, and unseen by most everyone in their lives.

Annie, a sophomore, begins a relationship with Malik, a senior. Her friends encouraged this relationship because of his new red Slidebar phone that is "almost as nice as those Blackberry ones." Their first encounter is awkward. Annie, so intent on sleeping with him to get pregnant, can't see that he is interested in more than sex with her. Malik wants to get to know Annie.

A young girl named Keera, a transfer student, enters the play and brings with her a world of hope for Annie. She has a close, happy home life where they have a weekly game night. Keera has a strong relationship with God. The combination of Keera and Malik's influence guide Annie toward making positive, proactive choices in her life. Unfortunately, when Annie discovers Keera's life is a lie, she acts out by sleeping with her tattoo artist and, subsequently, finds herself pregnant from the encounter. One bad choice derails the rest of her life.

Character Description
Malik, 17–18

On his first date with Annie, Malik takes her to a clearing in the park, in the midst of their urban environment, finding a place where they can see the stars and the moonlight. He has his eye on getting to know Annie intimately, not just sexually. He searched out this place so that it would be special. He knows the names and locations of the constellations even though he can't see the sky from his bedroom window. He fears that people in the planes flying overhead are laughing at him because of his social standing. His mother is very sick, but the illness is never disclosed. His view on life is best stated in his own words: "The world is a beautiful place. If it knocks you loose, it's your job to hold it together." He graduates class valedictorian and plans on attending University of Iowa.

Given Circumstances
Who are they? Malik and Annie go to the same school. They are acquaintances.

Where are they? A clearing in a park in a very urban environment.
When does this take place? Contemporary.
Why are they there? They are on a first date.
What is the pre-beat? Annie kisses Malik hard and reaches for his zipper.

Questions

1. When did Malik first notice Annie?
2. What does he find attractive about her?
3. What are his expectations of this first date?
4. How long did he take to find the perfect spot?
5. Why did he think this clearing in the park was the right place?
6. How does he handle the tough, urban city around him?
7. When did he realize he wanted to get out of this environment?
8. Has Malik had a girlfriend before?
9. What are his favorite subjects in school?
10. What is his home life like?
11. Does he feel that taking care of his mother is a burden or a blessing?
12. Aside from getting out of this city, what does Malik want to achieve in life?
13. Does Malik talk differently with Annie than he does with his friends?
14. What is the objective behind this monologue?
15. Why does Malik say this to Annie—why not just walk away or sleep with her?

Six Degrees of Separation
John Guare

RICK

He told me he had some of his own money and he wanted
to treat me. We went to a store that rented tuxedos and we
dressed to the nines. We went to the Rainbow Room. We
danced. High over New York City. I swear. He stood up
and held out my chair and we danced and there was a stir.
Nothing like this ever happened in Utah. And we danced.
And I'll tell you nothing like that must ever have happened
at the Rainbow Room because we were asked to leave. I tell
you. It was so funny.

And we walked out and walked home and I knew Elizabeth was waiting for me and I would have to explain about
the money and calm her down because we'll get it back but
I forgot because we took a carriage ride in the park and he
asked me if he could fuck me and I had never done anything
like that and he did and it was fantastic. It was the greatest
night I ever had and before we got home he kissed me on
the mouth and he vanished.

Later I realized he had no money of his own. He had
spent my money—our money—on that night at the Rainbow Room.

How am I going to face Elizabeth? What have I done? What did I let him do to me? I wanted experience. I came here to have experience. But I didn't come here to do this or lose that or be this or do this to Elizabeth. I didn't come here to be *this*. My father said I was a fool and I can't have him be right. What have I done?

Analysis: *Six Degrees of Separation*

Type: Dramatic
Synopsis

Chaos. Control. Chaos. Control. Flan and Ouisa Kittredge appear to have it all. Comfortably tucked away in their lavish Manhattan apartment, they maintain a safe distance from the darker, seedier side of the world. Then one evening Paul, a young African American man, bursts into their apartment bleeding from a knife wound to his side and sending Flan and Ouisa into a chaotic search for the truth—not only about Paul, but about themselves.

Paul claims to be the son of famed actor-director Sidney Poitier. He claims to attend Harvard University with the Kittredge children. He claims he was mugged in Central Park, the robbers taking his thesis and his money. He claims his father is making a movie version of the popular musical *Cats* and that he can cast Flan and Ouisa as extras. Paul is bright, charming, witty, and seemingly well educated. Paul is a fraud, a con man. Everything he says is a lie.

As Guare's story unfolds, we learn how Paul turned into a master manipulator. Trained by a boarding-school friend of the children, Paul quickly learned how to gain entry into their home. The Kittredge household is not his first. However, of all the houses he's conned his way into, Flan and Ouisa are the first to make him feel at home and really listen to what he has to say. They see Paul in a way no one has even tried to before. This, perhaps, is why Ouisa is so shaken by his deceit. Paul wanted to be them. He stabbed himself to get into their world. Her exploration of the situation leads her off track from the well-maintained, ordered world she has inhabited for so long.

Paul's lies have deadly consequences when a young man he meets commits suicide. Ouisa convinces Paul to turn himself in to the police, and he disappears into the prison system never to be seen or heard from again but leaving an undeniable imprint on Ouisa's life.

Character Description
Rick, mid-20s
Rick is a struggling actor, recently moved to New York City from Utah with his girlfriend, Elizabeth. They meet Paul while sitting in Central Park one afternoon, playing guitar. Rick tells Paul his dream roles are Uncle Vanya and Laertes in *Hamlet*.

Paul's lies lead them to invite him to live with them in their railroad apartment above a roller disco. He asks the young couple for money. They have very little, so Elizabeth says no. Rick goes behind her back and gives it to him.

After he recounts the events of their evening out, Rick throws himself out of his apartment window, committing suicide on Valentine's Day.

Given Circumstances
Who are they? Rick is talking to the audience. Maybe he is telling Flan and Ouisa or the police?
Where are they? New York City.
When does this take place? 1993.
Why are they there? Rick's world has been thrown into chaos by his encounter with Paul.
What is the pre-beat? Rick has realized Paul is a con man and a fraud.

Questions
1. What was Rick's life in Utah like?
2. How long has he been with Elizabeth? How did they meet?
3. Is he in love with Elizabeth?
4. What does New York feel like to Rick? How does it make him feel?
5. How is New York different than Utah?
6. Why does Rick want to act?
7. What is Rick's relationship to money? Has he ever had a lot?
8. What does Rick do to make money in NYC?
9. Did Rick know any homosexuals before Paul?
10. Why does he trust Paul with the money?
11. Where did he think the money for the night out came from?

12. Why is he telling this story?

13. Whom is he speaking to?

14. What is he hoping will happen when he relives this experience?

15. How does Rick deal with chaos?

Bachelorette
Leslye Headland

JOE

I went out drinking one night with my friend, Ethan. We'd been friends since, like, third grade. We got blasted. Stumbled back to my place and passed out in my bed. Lying side by side. He never woke up. He just never woke up. They said it was alcohol poisoning. But it turned out he had hepatitis too. So I don't know. He had started this whole heroin thing. Anyway . . . Maybe . . . there's something . . . he didn't look dead. You know? Even at the funeral, with the entire high school there, he just didn't look dead. It was like at any moment he was going to wake up and tell me I was a pussy for buying into this whole mourning and wearing black thing.

I wanted to just get high. I felt like that was what he would've wanted. Not all this eulogizing and sober bullshit. But my parents . . . it was crappy. I had to pretend to be this person who was really concerned. That's not the right word. But I had to be this, like, adult, or something. Why? You know? You can't just magically stop. Ethan fucking never woke up but it doesn't make me magically turn into someone who doesn't smoke or drink or get high or whatever. I resent that shit. Like the so-called "wake up" call. What the

fuck? Ethan lucked out. When they put him in the ground,
I knew he'd gotten away with it.

He never . . . he never had to grow up. I know that's
fucked up. But I feel like whatever . . . it's one of those
nights, right?

Analysis: *Bachelorette*

Type: Dramatic
Synopsis

Leslye Headland's dark comedy explores the tensions, jealousies,
and petty rivalries that exist among four female friends. All of these
feelings are especially heightened by the fact that Becky, the overweight and least popular friend, is getting married the next day to
a rich, successful, handsome man. Her three "friends" deal with
their jealousy by escaping into a night of alcohol, drugs, and sex.

Becky has asked Regan to be a bridesmaid even though the
two are no longer close. She has even asked Regan to spend the
night in her bridal suite on the condition that Regan not invite
Katie and Gena. Regan, of course, does just this.

Regan is a perfectionist and the queen bee of the group. Seemingly perfect on the outside, she is dependent on numerous prescription medications. Three years into a long-term relationship,
Regan can't understand why she's not the first to get married.
Gena is the sexiest of the group and, in many ways, the most mature. She is struggling to recover from a recent breakup. Katie is
the true beauty of the three. She is utterly lost. Still working retail
since graduation, she seems to have no real goal in life. She has

no relationship. She regularly drinks to the point of blacking out. On this particular evening, she mixes the booze with marijuana and cocaine in an almost deadly combination.

All three of these girls are searching for love but are unable to accept when a man is truly interested in them. This fact is illustrated by the interactions we see between them and Jeff and Joe, two men they pick up and bring back to the hotel. Both are nice guys, but nice guys finish last with these ladies.

Becky has learned to be mean from these girls. She has learned to manipulate. The deterioration of the evening culminates in a standoff between Becky and Regan that is simultaneously chilling and heartbreaking. These girls are not, and have never been, friends.

Character Description
Joe, 20s

Joe is a nice, normal guy. He meets this rowdy group of girls while out one night with his friend Jeff.

Joe finds himself falling harder than expected for Katie, and that's one of the reasons he's able to tell her this story. Joe likes to party. He likes to drink and do drugs. He likes to flirt and have sex with pretty women. There's something damaged about Katie that he recognizes and finds himself drawn to. He finds himself taking care of her in her blacked-out state when he could and should leave her with her friends.

Headland tells us very little about Joe, but his words speak much louder than his actions. He is a gentle, caring, kind young man who wants to protect Katie.

Given Circumstances

Who are they? Virtual strangers, Katie and Joe have just met tonight.

Where are they? The bridal suite of the Plaza Hotel, New York.

When does this take place? Contemporary.

Why are they there? Katie has picked him up and brought him back for a good time.

What is the pre-beat? Katie confesses to Joe that, a year ago, she tried to cut her wrists with a bottle.

Questions

1. How close are Jeff and Joe?
2. What does Joe find attractive about Katie?
3. How old was he when Ethan died?
4. Does he really believe Ethan got away with something?
5. What is Joe afraid of?
6. Why does he party so hard?
7. What is Joe's socioeconomic background?
8. How does he relate to these high-class surroundings?
9. Does he think Katie is obtainable?
10. Has Joe ever had a serious relationship?
11. What is he looking for in a woman?
12. What does Joe want from life?
13. Why does he tell Katie this story?
14. Just before this, Joe admits he was obsessed with Marilyn Monroe and the darkness that lurks behind the "perfect" image of her. What is he really saying to Katie?
15. What is the urgency behind this story?

Hit the Wall
Ike Holter

CLIFF

You're right, hey, you're right, cause if the pigs catch you, right here, right now,

you're going to jail, it's over, you're life's fucked forever. I know.

. . . If I get caught? I get on a plane. And they send me over there.

And I go, into the jungle, and the patties, and the black and I die.

And I will die. Guys in my family? We don't win war, we die, but I. Don't. Care.

Because if if they bust in and take us right now? Least I did what I wanted to do,

Now allright, I have no clue what it's like to be you-

But long as I'm around?

Fuck what the pigs say, fuck what Jackie-O-lameass says, fuck all of that noise—

We're gonna do whatever the hell we want.

. . . Cause we're gonna meet Judy Garland.

See, I've been up and down that block, people all over, everywhere but there,

see it, right down the block, big old cellar, smoked a J
right inside of it,

and down, down, down that cellar,

there's a hallway, there's steps, and there's a door,

and

I was sniffing around?

And right to the left of that door there's a hallway. And
round the corner

from that there's another door.

Behind that other door?

I heard music.

If you let me take you back there . . . will you let me
take you to a bar?

And let you let me let you let me buy you a drink?

Sorry, will you let someone buy me a drink which I will
then give to you because god-damn lady, you're worth it.

Analysis: *Hit the Wall*

Type: Dramatic
Synopsis

Ike Holter's *Hit the Wall* is an exploration of the chaos surrounding the Stonewall riots in New York City on the evening of June
27, 1969.

In this fictional account, Holter paints very specific portraits
of the misfits, the gays, the straights, the lesbians, and the cops
that collided that day. The play pulses with passion, fear, politics,
and humanity.

The story of Cliff and Carson is the heart of the play. Carson is an African American drag queen. He is dressed up in his finest to pay respects to his hero, Judy Garland, whose funeral is happening on the Upper East Side of Manhattan that day. Cliff is a Caucasian drifter and draft dodger. Cliff spotted Carson earlier in the day and now, coming across him once again, approaches him in hopes that they can share an evening together.

This unlikely pairing reflects the kind of stereotyping that Holter sets up and then strips down over the course of the play. No one is just what he or she seems on the surface. The misfits reject other outcasts. The nice, middle-aged straight woman rejects any showing of homosexuality on her block. The nice cop can wield his baton with strength and precision.

Holter places a live band onstage to heighten the pulse that charged that particular time in the late 1960s. Something was getting ready to break open, and it does so, explosively, in this play. Each character has so much at stake in a time when they're not allowed to be who they really want to be in an open, accepting environment.

Character Description
Cliff, 20s
A draft dodger with the hopes of being a world explorer, his actual travels have only gotten him to Iowa, Ohio, New Jersey, and, now, New York.

He is drunk on hope. He believes the world can and will be a better place one day. He believes there is a place for everyone. He believes in the half pound of amazing weed in his backpack.

He's been in trouble before, and he knows how to move fast in order to escape it.

Cliff is gay. He saw Carson today and "had to know what could happen. Had to know who the hell that was. For the first time, maybe." The rest gets cut off, but what is left unsaid is certainly charged with sex and hope. Cliff believes in the power of possibility.

Given Circumstances

Who are they? Carson is a drag queen. He and Cliff have just met.
Where are they? New York City's Upper East Side in front of Judy Garland's wake.
When does this take place? New York City, 1969.
Why are they there? To see Judy Garland's body before burial.
What is the pre-beat? Cliff has told Carson he saw him tell off some young thugs earlier in the day and is attracted to him.

Questions

1. Where is Cliff from originally?
2. Does he keep in contact with his family?
3. Do they know he's gay and a draft dodger?
4. With race relations being tense in the 1960s, how is it to be attracted to an African American drag queen?
5. What is it, exactly, that Cliff finds attractive about Carson?
6. Is this Cliff's first time in New York City?
7. How is New York City different from his hometown?
8. What does Cliff want from Carson?
9. What does Cliff want from life?

10. Who is Judy Garland to Cliff?

11. What is urgent about this monologue?

12. How easy is it for Cliff to be out of the closet in 1969?

13. Why does he smoke marijuana?

14. Cliff's language is jagged, cautious, and uncertain. Why?

15. Is Cliff afraid of death?

Water by the Spoonful
Quiara Alegría Hudes

ELLIOT

My sister and I had the stomach flu, right? For a whole day we couldn't keep nothing down. Medicine, juice, anything we ate, it would come right back up. Your co-worker here took us to Children's Hospital.

It was wall-to-wall packed. Every kid in Philly had this bug. ERs were turning kids away. They gave us a flier about stomach flu and sent us home. Bright blue paper. Little cartoon diagrams. It said give your kids a spoonful of water every five minutes.

A small enough amount that they can keep it down. Five minutes. Spoon. Five minutes. Spoon. I remember thinking, Wow, this is it. Family time. Quality time. Just the three of us. Because it was gentle, the way you said. "Open up." I opened my mouth, you put that little spoon of water into my mouth. That little bit of relief. And then I watched you do the same thing with my little sister. And I remember being like, "Wow, I love you, Mom. My moms is all right." Five minutes. Spoon. Five minutes. Spoon. But you couldn't stick to something like that. You couldn't sit there like that. You had to have your thing. That's where I stopped remembering.

A Department of Human Services report. That's my memory. Six hours later a neighbor kicks in the door. Me and my sister are lying in a pile of laundry. My shorts was all messed up. And what I really don't remember is my sister. Quote: "Female infant, approximately two years, pamper and tear ducts dry, likely cause of death, dehydration." Cuz when you dehydrate you can't form a single tear.

That's some friend you got there.

Analysis: *Water by the Spoonful*

Type: Dramatic
Synopsis

Elliot Ortiz is a disabled Iraqi war veteran who finds himself home in Philadelphia, working at Subway and pursuing a career as an actor. His life is thrown further off balance when his aunt Ginny, who raised him as a son, dies. Elliot's birth mother, Odessa, is a recovering heroin addict and she runs an online chat room, a safe world, for other addicts to meet, connect, and help each other stay sober. Yazmin, Elliot's cousin, is an adjunct professor of music dealing with the recent breakup of her marriage.

Hudes's play deals with everyone's struggle to find a safe space, to find a home. Odessa, a terrible mother to Elliot, has an online personality that totally contrasts his experiences with her. Her work as a janitor leaves her with little money and unable to really contribute to her sister's funeral. Elliot says very hurtful things to her that propel her to return to heroin after seven years clean.

Her relapse forces her into the hospital with no one but a stranger to take care of her as Elliot and Yaz fly to Puerto Rico to scatter Ginny's ashes into a waterfall at El Yunque. There, Yaz decides to buy the family home in North Philadelphia and Elliot resolves to pursue his dream and move to Los Angeles.

Character Description
Elliot, 24

Elliot dreams of being an actor. He works at a Subway half an hour away from his home so that his neighborhood friends don't see him there. He has filmed a few television commercials, but not enough to make a living off of. Elliot is haunted by the ghost of an Arabic man who repeats a mysterious phrase over and over again. Physically, he has a limp after undergoing four surgeries and, subsequently, battling his own addiction to painkillers.

Family is very important to Elliot. He loves Yaz dearly. They are very close, but he kept his addiction a secret from her. Elliot feels like he owes everything to Ginny. When his birth mother, Odessa, refuses to do her part, he actively punishes her by shaming her in public with the monologue included here. This is a merciless piece of writing; being family, Elliot knows how to push Odessa. He is aware that this speech might lead his mother into relapse. Elliot has a temper. He puts his fist through a wall when he learns of Ginny's death. When Odessa tells him to pawn her computer, her most prized possession, for money he first goes online, into Odessa's chat room, posing as her and mocking her work.

Ultimately, Elliot realizes the only road to happiness is to follow his dream, which means leaving Philadelphia and moving to Los Angeles.

Discussion

Given Circumstances
Who are they? Elliot, Yaz, Odessa, and a newly admitted addict.
Where are they? A diner in Philadelphia.
When does this take place? Contemporary.
Why are they there? Elliot and Yaz need money to buy flowers for Ginny's funeral.
What is the pre-beat? Odessa claims she has no money, no means of getting any, and cannot help. Yaz says she will pay for the flowers.

Questions
1. When did Elliot last see and spend time with his mother?
2. Having seen her online chat room, how does he feel about the persona she puts on there versus his actual experience of her?
3. What does family mean to Elliot?
4. Elliot calls Ginny his mom but Odessa by her given name; why?
5. Why did Elliot become a Marine?
6. How much fighting did he experience in Iraq?
7. Why is Elliot haunted by the ghost of an Arabic man?
8. Why does he want to be an actor?

9. How often does Elliot think of his deceased sister?
10. How was Elliot wounded in Iraq?
11. How did Elliot's addiction to painkillers affect his relationship with his mother?
12. Does Elliot fear his disability will impede his career?
13. What is Elliot scared of now?
14. Why hasn't Elliot moved to L.A. to pursue his dream?
15. What does "home" mean to him?

The Vandal
Hamish Linklater

BOY

Anyway Matt got like straight F's, he was always zonked out in the back of class, Zoloft probably, all in black like his dad, but ironically, I think, to piss his dad off, but so that's why — I mean I thought it even before I heard Tim Ross' mom say it — why Mrs. Bl-[2] chose Matt to get pregnant by, because Matt would never learn to say shit in French, not merde. But then, when she told him she was keeping it? Matt killed himself in that crazy way.

Self-entombment. That's what he died by: self-entombment. He buried himself alive.

It was kinda genius. There was a funeral that his dad was handling and he just swapped himself for the guy who was being buried. It was a closed casket deal, the dead guy, the already dead guy, Mr. Quinn I think, had died of some horrible like wasting disease, like Ebola of the head, and Matt's dad was like, "I can spruce him up and you can have the open casket but it'll cost you and arm and a leg

---

2   This is a self-edit by BOY. He doesn't want to disclose the teacher's full name in case the WOMAN knows her. He keeps forgetting and catching himself after he's started.

to fix his face," and the Quinn family, they were Catholic and poor, not unrelatedly, and Mrs. Quinn, formerly Fleischer, was still kinda young so maybe she wanted to save a little heading into the second chapter of her life, not Tim Ross' mom's favorite, Mrs. Quinn nee Fleischer, so they went closed casket, but then when Mr. Quinn, or maybe it was O'Keefe, anyway, when he was found in the woods by the road looking even more wasted, half eaten by woodland creatures and all, everyone wondered who they had just buried, cause the coffin definitely had a body in it, it was heavy. Imagine it, Matt had to just lay so still... So when they dug up the casket, it was too late of course, he'd suffocated, or just, I don't know what kills you in self-entombment, dehydration maybe, but at some point he had changed his mind because it was a mess in there, he'd torn at the insides of the lid, all the lining, the stuffing was torn out, and it stank of course because you lose control of your functions when you die, you literally lose your shit, but it was also supposed to be beautiful with him all covered in ripped out white stuffing – like he was laying in a cloud, or a bath of angel feathers.

I didn't really like Matt, I know tons of people who have died. This is Kingston.

Analysis: *The Vandal*

Type: Dramatic
Synopsis

On a cold winter's night in Kingston, New York, a Boy and a Woman meet at a bus stop situated in the center of a triangle whose points are made up of a hospital, a cemetery, and a liquor store. The bus stop functions as a kind of limbo, a meeting place for lost souls. The Vandal is a meditation on life and death, truth versus lies, family, parenthood, and marriage. Linklater explores all of these epic themes in this intimate, three-character play.

The unnamed Boy starts a conversation with the Woman at the bus stop. He is charming, disarming, blunt, and flirtatious. He opens up about his past and tells some horrific stories detailing life in the small upstate town. The Woman is somewhat guarded but, ultimately charmed by him, agrees to go to the liquor store and buy the Boy a six-pack of beer.

Things get complicated for the Woman when the owner of the liquor store turns out to be the Boy's father. We also discover that the Woman is using someone else's credit card to make her purchase. She pours out the story of her recently deceased husband and the nurse who took care of him at the nearby hospital. The line between truth and fantasy gets more blurred with each passing moment. What becomes very clear is that each of these three characters has suffered a great loss and is in pain. It is their pain that brings them together and makes their meeting seem somehow more than chance.

The Woman heads back to the Boy with the beer and chips. He leads her into the cemetery and disappears. The Man appears and reveals that the Boy died a year ago in a terrible car accident.

Character Description
Boy, teens
Kingston, New York, is a small upstate town that was once a center of activity. Now it is slow, sleepy, and somewhat decaying. The Boy has lived his entire life there.

He tells the Woman that his mother died in childbirth. He tells the Woman about the car accident that killed three of his classmates last year. He tells the story of the self-entombment of his classmate. He is obsessed with death.

When they first meet, the Boy questions the Woman intensely. He is smart. He is challenging. He is flirtatious. He is outgoing. He is well mannered. In the final scene, it is revealed that he is dead.

His name was Robert, according to his father. His mother did not die in childbirth. She left the family. He often sends people into the liquor store to buy beer for him, and his father, Man, knows that it's a way of keeping in touch with him without actually revealing himself.

Given Circumstances
Who are they? Strangers who have just met.
Where are they? A bus stop on a cold winter's night in Kingston, New York.
When does this take place? Contemporary.

Why are they there? The Woman is heading home, the Boy is hanging out.

What is the pre-beat? The Boy has told the Woman she reminds him of a teacher, Mrs. Bl-.

Questions

1. Late in the play, we discover the Boy is really dead. Why does he hang around?
2. What does life and death mean to the Boy?
3. What did he want from life?
4. What does he want in death?
5. Why does he talk to the Woman?
6. Why does he tell her this story?
7. Why doesn't the boy appear to his father, who owns the liquor store?
8. The Boy lies to the Woman about his mother. Why?
9. What was the Boy's relationship with his father like in life?
10. What was his socioeconomic background?
11. How does he feel about Matt choosing death, and then changing his mind?
12. What is life in a small town like for a teenaged boy?
13. Whom else has the Boy appeared to?
14. Does the Boy want the Woman to meet his father?
15. What is urgent about this monologue?

The Vandal
Hamish Linklater

BOY

You know what I like with Cool Ranch, any Dorito really, as opposed to like a Sun Chip? Or a, I don't know, regular tortilla chip? The flavor dust that gets stuck to your fingers when you bite your chip. See? With Cool Ranch it's like, a blue and gold flavor dust. It's not really the color of ranch dressing. Maybe it's a metaphor: "Cool Ranch". . . But then look at this: so like, you lick it off. The flavor dust. (*He licks his fingers*) Voila. But then when you go for the next chip, your fingers are like wet and sticky, so more flavor dust sticks to your fingers, so you lick em again, and your fingers get wetter and stickier, so there's gonna be more flavor dust, there's gonna be more licking, and eventually it'll just coat your fingers, your tongue and lips get all coated too, and who knows eventually if the licking is actually cleaning your fingers, or just shellacking on more layers of pasty flavor dust. It's just like this passing back and forth of smoosh that losing flavor. It's just this cleaning which isn't even tasting anymore, this cleaning that's only making a bigger mess. It's a negative feed back cycle. And the chip, the start of the whole thing, is like beside the point.

Do you think that's a metaphor?

Is, like, the chip our Life, the flavor dust our dreams, the fingers reality, they moosh together, and then your mouth is like death?

Or maybe the chip is your heart, the flavor dust is love, the fingers are heartbreak, and then time just gobbles them up?

Analysis: *The Vandal*

Type: Seriocomic
Synopsis

On a cold winter's night in Kingston, New York, a Boy and a Woman meet at a bus stop situated in the center of a triangle whose points are made up of a hospital, a cemetery, and a liquor store. The bus stop functions as a kind of limbo, a meeting place for lost souls. *The Vandal* is a meditation on life and death, truth versus lies, family, parenthood, and marriage. Linklater explores all of these epic themes in this intimate three-character play.

The unnamed Boy starts a conversation with the Woman at the bus stop. He is charming, disarming, blunt, and flirtatious. He opens up about his past and tells some horrific stories detailing life in the small upstate town. The Woman is somewhat guarded but, ultimately charmed by him, agrees to go to the liquor store and buy the Boy a six-pack of beer.

Things get complicated for the Woman when the owner of the liquor store turns out to be the Boy's father. We also discover that the Woman is using someone else's credit card to make her purchase. She pours out the story of her recently deceased husband

and the nurse who took care of him at the nearby hospital. The line between truth and fantasy gets blurred with each passing moment. What becomes very clear is that each of these three characters has suffered a great loss and is in pain. It is their pain that brings them together and makes their meeting seem somehow more than chance.

The Woman heads back to the Boy with the beer and chips. He leads her into the cemetery and disappears. The Man appears and reveals that the Boy died a year ago in a terrible car accident.

Character Description

Boy, teens

Kingston, New York, is a small upstate town that was once a center of activity. Now it is slow, sleepy, and somewhat decaying. The Boy has lived his entire life there.

He tells the Woman that his mother died in childbirth. He tells the Woman about the car accident that killed three of his classmates last year. He tells the story of the self-entombment of his classmate. He is obsessed with death.

When they first meet, the Boy questions the Woman intensely. He is smart. He is challenging. He is flirtatious. He is outgoing. He is well mannered. In the final scene, it is revealed that he is dead.

His name was Robert, according to his father. His mother did not die in childbirth. She left the family. He often sends people into the liquor store to buy beer for him, and his father, Man, knows that it's a way of keeping in touch with him without actually revealing himself.

Given Circumstances

Who are they? The Boy and Woman have just met tonight.

Where are they? A bus stop in Kingston, New York, on a cold winter's night.

When does this take place? Contemporary.

Why are they there? They have forged an unlikely companionship.

What is the pre-beat? The Woman has bought him beer and chips from his father's liquor store.

Questions

1. Late in the play, we discover the Boy is really dead: why does he hang around?
2. What do life and death mean to the Boy?
3. What did he want from life?
4. What does he want in death?
5. Why does he talk to the Woman?
6. What does he miss about living?
7. Why doesn't the boy appear to his father, who owns the liquor store?
8. The Boy lies to the Woman about his mother. Why?
9. What was the Boy's relationship with his father like in life?
10. What was his socioeconomic background?
11. How often does the Boy make human contact?
12. What is life in a small town like for a teenaged boy?
13. Whom else has the Boy appeared to?
14. Does the Boy want the Woman to meet his father?
15. Why is he going on and on about Doritos?

Ella
Dano Madden

CUTTER

My daddy. I seen the way he lookin' at the ladies. My momma's his third wife. I seen him. Lookin' at the ladies. Speakin' to the ladies like he a real nice man. Lots a things bad in what my daddy does, but that's the one that bother me the most. That's why my momma tells me to leave. She seen me lookin' at him. She knows the look. The way I stared at my daddy sometimes. (*Beat.*) Like I wanna put a bullet 'tween his eyes. (*Beat.*) My momma saw the look in my eyes. And, one time, my daddy, he saw it too. He saw me lookin' at him, at him speakin' to my Momma's sister. The way he's laughin' and treatin' her so nice. My daddy saw me. Didn't say nothin'. I knowed he saw me. He looked right at me. Middle of the night, he kickin' me to wake me up. He and my brothers. They all kickin' me. "Get up Cutter, get up." And they cursin', ma'am. Things I'd rather not say to you. No one in the world awake at this hour of the night. So I get up and they shove me outside. And we in the truck, drivin'. Humid night. Hotter than usual. I asked where we goin' and daddy says we goin' out gator huntin'. We drive and we drive out to Lake Okeechobee. It's a real big lake. Daddy park the truck and my brothers throw me in the boat. They real strong, my brothers.

Muscles from farmin'. My daddy steers us out, real near where he like to hunt gators. And he stops the boat. The night is so quiet. I never heard a night this quiet. My brothers pick me up and hold me over the water. And daddy says, Pardon me ma'am, but, "Who the f— do you think you are? You gotta problem with your daddy gettin' a little action? Your brothers don't mind." And they still holdin' me out over the lake. "No woman gonna tell me what to do. Not your momma. No one. You look at me like you think you so good. You look at me like I'm a, he used the "n" word ma'am. He use that word a lot. I'm sorry for that ma'am. He told me I looking at him like he were a "n." And my brothers throw me in the water. In the lake. I can't see nothin'. I started cryin' like a girl. I thinkin' about what's in the water with me. I try to swim to the boat, and my brothers push me away, kick at me. My daddy says to me, yells, "You gonna look at me like a "n" again?" And I yell no Daddy! Please let me back in the boat. And I out in the water, feels like a long long time. Forever. Finally, my brothers, they grab me up out the water and throw me back in the boat. My daddy says, "You look at me like that again and I leave you out here." And that's the end a that.

Discussion

Type: Dramatic
Synopsis
Ella is a twenty-nine-year-old African American sculptor who has recently relocated to Seattle, Washington. She lives in the

upstairs bedroom of her younger sister Vanessa's house. Vanessa is a student at the University of Washington. Ella is trying to escape a recent personal tragedy: her ex-husband, who cheated on her with a younger woman, killed himself. Ella blames herself for his death, because she refused to get back together with him when he sought forgiveness.

The action of the play takes place over the course of one evening. Vanessa is throwing a party in her downstairs apartment. She desperately wants Ella to come down, socialize, and take her mind off of her problems. Ella wants to stay in her room and sculpt, but she is haunted by visions of her ex. Cutter, a nineteen-year-old Florida farm boy, who wanders up to her room in order to escape the party, also interrupts Ella.

Cutter is also escaping his father, who showed up on his doorstep to take him back to Florida. His father is unaware that Cutter has enlisted in the military and is scheduled to show up for basic training the next day. Despite some initial high tensions, Ella and Cutter discover they share many things in common and, over a short period of time, open up to each other in unexpected ways.

Character Description
Cutter, 19
Cutter is a Florida farm boy, the youngest of four children (he has three older half brothers), and his mother's favorite child. His mother, sensing something different about him, spent Cutter's entire life persuading him to get out of Okeechobee. She knew he didn't fit in with his father and brothers. Cutter had dreams of staying there, building a house on his daddy's property, "Nothing

huge, but nice. Hardwood floors. Two story high. Big windows. Wanted a little room upstairs to work in." That room upstairs was to write. That dream couldn't be, so he applied to a college and found himself at the University of Washington, unable to afford it. The only way for him to stay away from Okeechobee was to enlist. Eventually the government will pay for his education, and in the meantime, he will be free.

It's important to Cutter that people don't mistake him and his beliefs for those of his family. Ella is put off when he admits his father is racist. She believes he must be as well, and this mono-logue springs up as a reaction to her resistance to him.

Given Circumstances

Who are they? Strangers who have only just met.

Where are they? Ella's bedroom in an apartment in Seattle, Washington.

When does this take place? Contemporary.

Why are they there? Cutter is escaping his father as well as the party downstairs.

What is the pre-beat? Ella believes Cutter to be racist like his Daddy and orders him to leave her room.

Questions

1. Why doesn't Cutter tell his father that he's joining the military?
2. Why does Cutter leave the party and venture up to Ella's room?

3. Why does Cutter stay so long even after Ella demands that he leaves?

4. What does Cutter want from Ella?

5. What does Cutter write: fiction, nonfiction, short stories?

6. Why does Cutter write?

7. Has Cutter ever found a place where he feels he belongs?

8. Is Cutter attracted to Ella?

9. He is very moved by Ella's sculptures. Why do they touch him so much?

10. How did Cutter survive all those years at home?

11. Cutter says his daddy isn't all bad. What are some good things about the man?

12. How does Cutter feel about enlisting tomorrow?

13. What does Cutter love about Okeechobee?

14. What does Cutter love about college?

15. What is urgent about this monologue?

The Four of Us
Itamar Moses

DAVID

So, right, like you said, I've been seeing this girl.

Okay. We're lying in bed together, you know . . . after . . . and we're going to sleep, and I just have this thought, this one, stray, like, rogue, thought, just creeps in, just sort of flits across my brain, and the thought is this: What if I feel absolutely nothing for this person?

That was it. That was the thought. What if I feel nothing? And suddenly. I mean. It was like my heart . . . stopped. Or like I fell through ice. Or like. If my life was a movie? Like I was the hero, and I had *won*, I got the girl, you know, and the credits rolled, and, but, instead of it being over, and me being allowed to get up and, you know, *leave*, instead I was still stuck in the movie, and, even worse, everybody around me still believed the movie was real, and was still in character, and I had to, like, play along, but with no actual sentiment behind it, I mean, seriously, I just wanted to turn to her right there, in the dark, and say, "Hey. Remember when I said I loved you? What a great scene *that* was. Okay! That's a wrap! Maybe we'll work together again someday!" Only I can't do that. I mean: obviously. I mean: I don't want to *want* to. Because until like a second before that, literally

like a second before, everything felt so . . . good. Just . . .
fine. And then I have this one thought and everything just,
like, inverted, like a photo negative, or . . . And not just with
this girl, but suddenly I started seeing everything this way.
From that moment. I, literally, I have been literally divid-
ing my life, you know, mentally, into the moment before I
had that thought and the moment after I had that thought.
This one . . . *thought*. And I . . .

Are you even *listening* to me?

Analysis: *The Four of Us*

Type: Dramatic
Synopsis

David and Benjamin are best friends. Itamar Moses's play charts
the trajectory of their relationship from the ages of seventeen to
twenty-seven. David is a playwright, Benjamin a novelist. In a series of scenes, alternating in time and location, Moses illustrates
how little cuts can become big wounds over the course of time.
Benjamin's career takes off to an astronomical level, leaving David
to struggle seemingly alone.

The tension between David and Benjamin is evident in most
every scene save for the last, which takes place at summer camp
when the two are seventeen years old, just about to embark on
their journey.

In the startling penultimate scene, Moses reveals that what we
have been watching is a play, written by David, about his relationship with the now very successful Benjamin. Everything we have

been watching/reading has been filtered through David's point of view. Benjamin storms out, and the two have a confrontation in the theater lobby, but David convinces Benjamin to go back in and watch the final scene, which is the same scene we see: the two young boys at summer camp.

Character Description
David, 20

David is a playwright. He has watched his friend Benjamin's career skyrocket after selling his book and the film rights for two million dollars at the age of twenty-four.

At the age of nineteen, the two go to Prague together. Benjamin spends day and night writing while David parties. During this time, David gets an idea for a play and writes a very bad draft of it that goes nowhere until he uncovers it years later.

David seems indifferent in his relationships with women, while Benjamin stays committed to whomever he is with. In fact, David says relationships make him feel "emotional claustrophobia" and that he suffers from "inexplicable depression" and "anxiety attacks" when in them.

Over the course of the play, David struggles to keep his bitterness in control while expressing happiness for Benjamin's success. Even when Benjamin asks David to write the film treatment of his book for a famous movie star, David finds a way to turn a positive situation on its head. David is the yang to Benjamin's yin. Moses brilliantly illustrates how and why the two are friends, but tension courses underneath their relationship at every turn.

Given Circumstances

Who are they? Best friends.

Where are they? Benjamin's dorm room.

When does this take place? Contemporary.

Why are they there? David is visiting Benjamin at school.

What is the pre-beat? David is trying to convince Benjamin to go to a party.

Questions

1. Why are Benjamin and David friends?
2. How are they similar/different?
3. What does David write about?
4. Does David have a writing schedule?
5. Who are David's playwriting influences?
6. What does "writing" really mean to David?
7. What does "success" mean to David?
8. Why is David unable to commit to a romantic relationship?
9. How long do David's romantic relationships tend to last?
10. How do they tend to end?
11. Who is this girl in the monologue?
12. How did they meet?
13. What does she look like?
14. How long have they been dating?
15. What is urgent about this monologue?

Jailbait
Deirdre O'Connor

MARK

My brother got engaged this summer. I'm supposed to be his best man, if you can imagine that. And I'll admit, when he called me up my first reaction was, "ah fuck," right? There he goes. There goes my brother to a life of fucking Netflix every night and matching Banana Republic outfits. So I'm not even hearing what he's saying. Talking about picking out the ring. Talking about the fucking five Cs of diamonds as if I give a fuck. And I am depressed, you know. My little brother. This hits me hard. And I'm actually sitting there wallowing, not even realizing that he's happy. I mean off-his-balls happy. That this is exactly what he wants.

So I fucked his fiancée. Joke. Just a joke. His fiancée's fucking ugly.

I'm writing a toast to this marriage. This marriage I dread. This death of my brother as I've known him and I'm toasting to it.

I'm an asshole. I know it at least. I'm not the enemy. I'm not twisting my moustache trying to keep you single. But you've been low and I don't know how to help you. If you want to call her, call her. If you are stupid for Valerie in a

way that I was too dense to see, I will write the fucking toast.
Just tell me what you want.

Analysis: *Jailbait*

Type: Seriocomic
Synopsis

On the surface, *Jailbait* is the story of two high-school-aged girls
who pretend to be older in order to get into a Boston nightclub.
Once there, they split up and have two very different evenings
with two older, more experienced men. Deirdre O'Connor's play
is, however, intent on digging deep under the surface of these
characters to show that looks are deceiving and age and maturity
don't necessarily travel hand in hand. A meditation on "growing
up," O'Connor's play is funny, painful, eye-opening, and sad.

Claire, fifteen years old, is still coping with the death of her
father when she is forced to deal with the fact her mother has
started dating. She reconnects with her friend Emmy, the same
age but seemingly more experienced. Emmy dresses Claire up,
does her makeup, and takes her out to a nightclub where she has
two men waiting for them: Robert and Mark.

Robert is coping with the recent breakup of his long-term relationship with Val. Mark is taking Robert out to help him forget
about Val and move on with his life. Mark is convinced Robert
was in love with the idea of Val much more than the actual person.

Claire and Robert find in each other kindred spirits. They share
a genuine affinity, despite their age difference. They go home together, and Claire loses her virginity to him. Meanwhile, a scared

Emmy confesses their real ages to Mark. Her night with him totally backfires, and he is forced to run to Robert's place to tell him the truth about the girls. In the climactic scene, Claire and Robert are forced to deal with what has happened between them and come to terms with the situation. Ultimately, Claire realizes that there is no one event that facilitates growing up, but rather a series of events that lead to emotional growth and psychological maturity.

Character Description
Mark, mid–late 20s
Although a self-proclaimed "asshole," Mark is, at the same time, completely self-aware.

Functioning in a state of self-protection after a bad breakup with Jennifer, the details of which are never defined, Mark keeps his relationships with women casual, playful, and strictly physical.

Mark is successful. He works hard and plays hard. While he may be reticent to accept love into his own life, he is not blind to those in his life who have found it. This monologue is a wonderful reflection of that. Mark's realization that his brother is, in fact, in love with his fiancée allows him to see that Robert was never really in love with Val.

Mark immediately ends his flirtation with Emmy when he finds out her actual age. Under his armor, he is a caring person. His final confrontation with Robert leads him to realize just how much growing up he still has yet to do.

Given Circumstances
Who are they? Best friends.

Where are they? The bathroom of a Boston nightclub.

When does this take place? Contemporary.

Why are they there? To distract Robert from his broken heart.

What is the pre-beat? Mark finds Robert checking his phone for a message from Val.

Questions

1. How long have Mark and Robert been friends?
2. What do they have in common?
3. Who was Jennifer, and what were the circumstances surrounding their relationship?
4. How did Mark's relationship with Jennifer end?
5. How did the end of this relationship fuel the way Mark acts now?
6. What are Mark's opinions about Val?
7. Robert accuses Mark of living a "miserable life." Does Mark see it that way?
8. Is Mark close to his brother?
9. What does it mean to be the older brother watching your younger brother marry?
10. What does Mark really think about his brother's fiancée?
11. What are Mark's opinions about marriage?
12. What's wrong with a life of Banana Republic and Netflix every night?
13. What would Mark's wedding toast say?
14. Where does Mark picture himself in five years? Ten?
15. Does Mark ever dream of a regular, married, stable life?

Wild
Crystal Skillman

PETER

My father. He's sick.

He's really fucking sick. Sure you can say it's prostate cancer but it's not even just one thing—drinking like—and his body is literally falling apart. Has been. Piece by piece. Not that he gives a shit.

When I brought Bobby home? I didn't prepare them. We just walked in. As if we could walk in and everything would be ok. Bobby had no idea—he's just like, "They're shit, forget them!" Bobby's family they're—they love him.

Bobby's mom and dad, his brother Ted rally around him like—and mine? My sister Ellen tells me I'm going to hell. She doesn't say those words but she leaves reports of misery on my phone. Sends photos of dear old dying dad.

Today's message? "This is it."

So I fucking have patience. I get it together. I take my lunch break.

I go to the hospital.

I can't get past the doors. I look at them and other people going in and out and I know I'm on some list— like "don't let him in" but I know if I wanted to—if I want—they couldn't stop me—but it's me—I can't go in

there—me—so—so—here's the thing—I you asked my family to cut me up and said to my fucked up dying father what
part of your son do you like? What one fucking thing of your
son—what redeeming quality do you love? He wouldn't
pick any part of me. They wouldn't pick any part of me. I
hurt them because of who I am. I hurt Bobby—I fucked
someone else. A woman. I don't know why. I fucked it up.
And I'm telling you this because I hurt people and I don't
know why. I can't change what I did and I can't fix it. I'm
just trying and it's not good enough. Not any piece of me
is good enough and I don't know what to do.

Analysis: *Wild*

Type: Dramatic
Synopsis

Peter and Bobby have been a couple for four years. They work
together at Mesirow, a large Chicago-based financial institution.
They also live together but keep their relationship a secret from
their co-workers. The play begins with Peter on the shore of Lake
Michigan about to have sex with a young woman named Nikki.
The two have just met and Peter says very little except, "Don't
use my name."

Every scene in WILD takes place along the shore. The ebb and
flow of the tide mirrors the push and pull of Peter and Bobby's
relationship. Skillman deftly explores how Peter's cheating affects
the couple as well as the other people in their lives. Peter and
Bobby kind of break up but still live together. Bobby begins an

affair with an office intern, Jordy. Peter begins a new relationship with Vin, a man he meets on the beach. Vin is the recipient of Peter's monologue, and it happens upon their first meeting. There is an intimacy that Peter can share with this stranger that he can't share with his longtime lover.

Bobby's family has become very close to Peter over the years. Peter officially came out when he met them. Ted, Bobby's brother, works at the hospital where Peter's father is deteriorating and tells Peter, who still can't make it through the doors, that the family plans to take Peter's father off of life support. The more the characters' lives spin out of control in this play, the more "wild" they act. Eventually, Peter and Bobby lose their jobs as well as their new lovers but find themselves reconnecting and reigniting their relationship.

Character Description
Peter, 25

Skillman describes Peter as "Bobby's boyfriend. Explosive, highly insecure underneath." It isn't until six months after the indiscretion that Peter tells Bobby about it. The spot on the beach where Peter had sex with Nikki is also Peter and Bobby's favorite spot. The location is charged with meaning. Peter tells Bobby while they're out shopping. He uses the excuse that Bobby wanted "honesty" from him. In fact, Peter doesn't know what he wants anymore. He's unhappy at work, unhappy in his relationship, and unhappy with his family. The fact that his father is dying and they have so many unresolved issues between them pushes Peter further into despair, causing him to act out.

Peter attempts to make amends with Bobby after the confession, but Bobby won't hear of it at first. Peter tried to let Bobby in, tries to comfort him, but Bobby is too hurt to forgive. And so Peter goes out and finds comfort in the arms of Vin. But Peter isn't ready for a new relationship, and Vin quickly realizes that.

Peter and Bobby reconnect on the beach, at their spot. They admit that they can't imagine their lives without each other and that "love is wild."

Given Circumstances

Who are they? Peter and Vin have just met.

Where are they? The shoreline of Lake Michigan in Chicago.

When does this take place? Contemporary.

Why are they there? Peter is having "lunch" (an energy drink) on the beach.

What is the pre-beat? Vin says, "It's easier to tell a stranger . . . why you act pissed but look like you're going to cry."

Questions

1. What does Peter want from life?
2. What does Peter want from his father? His family?
3. Why can't Peter cross the threshold and go into his father's room?
4. Could Peter see his father in the room? If so, what did he look like?
5. What does Bobby look like?
6. What aspects or qualities of Bobby did Peter fall in love with?

7. Which of these aspects does he still love?
8. What did Peter get out of sleeping with Nikki?
9. Why did Peter wait so long to tell Bobby he slept with Nikki?
10. What does Peter open up to Vin in a way he can't to Bobby?
11. What does Vin look like?
12. What does Peter want from Vin?
13. What draw does this particular shoreline have for Peter?
14. Why does Peter not like his job?
15. What is urgent about this monologue?

Victoria Martin: Math Team Queen
Kathryn Walat

JIMMY

OK, *this* is the big game. In case you don't remember, every school year there is *the game*. And this is that game—bigger than homecoming, bigger than the Thanksgiving game or any other football thing. It's bigger than Sanjay Patel's totally, unbelievable awesome final Math Team meet before he moved to Arizona. Bigger than any of the Chess Team matches—I know, I'm on the team—bigger than the swim meet when Bruce Owen was standing on the starting block with a total boner—*bigger* than Bruce Owen's boner—this is the basketball State Championship game. And we were in it. And I was doing the stats. And Scott Sumner—even though he is only a *junior* and no one even *knew* his name last year—is totally, totally awesome.

And really nice to me too. Like, whenever Scott Sumner sees me, he says: Hey Jimmy. And he means me. And he *really* means it. And that makes me feel like when my mom wakes me up on Saturday morning sometimes—like she did this morning, because it was a big day because I was going to do stats for the big game—and she says: Guess who's getting blueberry muffins with maple syrup? And she means *me*.

The guys on the team were so nervous in the locker room that some of them started praying. And the cheerleaders must have been nervous too because someone said they were all throwing up in the girl's locker room. And the whole team shaved their heads.

Even second-string. But I think some of them wished they didn't now, like one of the point guards, who has really bad acne in his hairline, except now there's no hairline, so it's just a line of zits.

And the cheerleaders were all going to get their legs waxed. I don't really know why they'd do that, but I guess it's something that hurts, and the second-string forward said he thought that showed solidarity. Well, he didn't use that word, solidarity, but I was listening to the whole conversation, sitting there at my little card table next to the bench, and I know what he meant.

Victoria Martin is sitting in the stands right in the middle of our section, right where she always sits. She looks *so beautiful*. And when Scott Sumner runs in at the front of the tunnel run, while they play that music that makes everyone get up and shake their butts—he always looks up to the stands, right to that spot, and I know he's looking for her. And their eyes meet. And every game I think: Wow, that's love.

Analysis: *Victoria Martin: Math Team Queen*

Type: Comedic
Synopsis

Victoria Martin is a popular high school sophomore. Her two best friends—the Jens—are varsity cheerleaders. Her boyfriend, Scott Sumner, is a junior and the varsity first swing on the basketball team.

The Math Team is suffering debilitating losses after its star player, Sanjay Patel, moved to Arizona. At the prodding of her math teacher, Mr. Riley, Victoria secretly shows up to a Math Team meeting. She loves numbers. She's good with them. Victoria's parents are in the middle of a divorce, and her father has moved across the country, to California. A love of math and numbers is something she shares with her dad. Being on the Math Team is a way for Victoria to stay close to him.

However, being on the Math Team also puts Victoria's popularity at great risk. The Jens would never understand. She would be labeled a geek. She creates a series of lies and evasions to explain her sudden change in schedule to the Jens and to Scott. The consequences extend beyond this. Victoria finds herself kissing Peter, a fellow team member, on the night of Scott's big game, and word quickly spreads when Jimmy, a freshman with a huge crush on Victoria, sees the kiss and reports it immediately.

Victoria Martin: Math Team Queen is a touching, funny, and honest look at the roles we're assigned in high school, sometimes outside of our control, and how we can maneuver them to our advantage or even redefine ourselves.

Victoria discovers that the personal happiness and rewards she finds as a member of the Math Team outweigh those of just being popular.

Character Description
Jimmy, 14–15

Jimmy is a high school freshman. Smart, eager, and maybe a little geeky, Jimmy is looking for his place. He enjoys being a member of the Math Team and is floored when the very popular sophomore Victoria Martin, appears on the team. He falls madly in love with her, not only because of who she is, but also because of her popularity. He also has the job of keeping statistics for the basketball team.

Jimmy is so devastated when he finds Victoria kissing fellow team member Peter during the big game that he wets his pants and runs directly to the field and tells Victoria's boyfriend, varsity basketballer Scott Sumner.

Given Circumstances

Who are they? Jimmy is talking directly to the audience.
Where are they? At the season's biggest basketball game.
When does this take place? Contemporary.
Why are they there? It's the biggest game of the year. Everyone is there.
What is the pre-beat? The first half of the game has just ended.

Questions

1. What does "popularity" mean to Jimmy?
2. What does he find attractive about Victoria?
3. When does he feel like he "fits in"?
4. What does keeping statistics for the basketball team entail?
5. Does keeping statistics make him feel as if he's part of the team?
6. Why is Scott Sumner's attention so important to him?
7. What does he like about the Math Team other than Victoria?
8. What does it mean to be a freshman?
9. What does "love" mean to Jimmy?
10. Has he ever been in love before?
11. Does Jimmy have many friends?
12. What does Jimmy do for fun?
13. What's Jimmy's relationship with his father?
14. What comfort does Jimmy find in numbers?
15. What is urgent about this monologue?

Women's Monologues

The Drunken City
Adam Bock

MARNIE

I'm not kissing you in a church. I got more important things
to figure out. Be serious.

You gotta help me figure this out. Please?

I wanted the wedding. Because it's gonna be a gorgeous
wedding. I'm gonna wear my Mom's wedding dress

it's from 1910 and her Mom wore it

and her mom's mom wore it

and it's satin with inlaid pearls, well not inlaid pearls,
that's not the word I'm, and I remember when I was a tiny
little girl I remember thinking "I'm gonna wear that dress"
because it's the most, it's gorgeous and I'm gonna get to be
looked at, I'm gonna,

Gary was just a prop. He was. He was just

And I knew he wanted me to say yes, so I did. I just

I kept lying

And then, worse, Frank, worse, he suddenly changed
on me.

He started acting like a husband. How he thinks a husband is, the world's dangerous and he has to protect me
and that means I have to listen to him and he's gonna tell
me what to do and I'm gonna have to act like he tells me.

He's gonna be like his Dad. But his Mom's this little mousy woman who never says Boo.

And I'm not gonna be her.

Uh uh.

But I just don't know what to say to Gary.

I want to tell him the truth. I do.

It's good you brought me here. I'm gonna need some help doing all this. Will you wait for me? I'm gonna go sit and be quiet for a minute. You're so sweet. I wish I'd met you before I met Gary.

Analysis: *The Drunken City*

Type: Seriocomic
Synopsis

People meet. They fall in love. They get engaged. They get married. They live happily ever after. Or that's how it's supposed to happen. Adam Bock's play *The Drunken City* dissects the heart of relationships in that very tenuous time between engagement and marriage, exploring the many false justifications people create for such a sacred event.

In the first scene, three young women, all best friends, descend upon an unnamed city to celebrate the fact that they've all recently become engaged. Marnie is engaged to Gary. Melissa is engaged to Jason. Linda is engaged to Jack. Marnie and Melissa work together at the Sunshine Bakery. Linda comes in and eats the muffins. All three are over the moon with excitement.

Fast-forward three weeks, the ladies are back in the city for Marnie's bachelorette party. Melissa has discovered that Jason was cheating on her, and she's no longer engaged. They have spent the day shopping for bridesmaids' dresses. Suddenly a drunken Marnie finds herself kissing a man, Frank, on the street. This event and numerous others over the course of the evening cause the entire world to, literally, tilt. Every time the world tilts, the characters slide from one side of the stage to the other or sometimes even on and off stage.

This drunken night causes Marnie to seriously question her relationship with Gary and her motivations for marrying him. Frank, recently out of his own long-term relationship, listens to Marnie in a way that no one else ever has. Melissa, still reeling over her breakup with Jason, refuses to let Marnie sabotage her relationship with Gary. She calls in their boss, Bob, to come and help talk some sense into Marnie. Bob has his own relationship problems, though, and doesn't really have the skills necessary to help. He finds himself falling unexpectedly for Frank's best friend, Eddie.

Bock's play is far from a condemnation of marriage or traditional relationships. He is, however, forcing the audience to approach these commitments with awareness of their partners as well as themselves. All of these characters reach a certain level of understanding because of the events of one drunken night.

Character Description
Marnie, mid-20s

Marnie works at the Sunshine Bakery with Melissa and Bob. Linda is a customer and one of her best friends. Marnie is engaged to marry Gary. At her bachelorette party she runs into Frank, who works at her bank. She finds herself sneaking kisses with him. Then the kisses get not-so-sneaky. Then the streets start to tilt and her whole world tilts, breaking the illusion of her perfectly planned future. She and Gary have plans to marry in a church. They have just bought a car together. They're talking about getting a dog, a breed that would be good with kids because they will eventually be having kids. Everything is all mapped out for her, until she kisses Frank.

Given Circumstances

Who are they? Marnie and Frank are acquaintances who are getting to know each other better.

Where are they? Inside a church.

When does this take place? The night of Marnie's bachelorette party.

Why are they there? They are falling for each other and trying to escape their friends.

What is the pre-beat? Frank has just tried to kiss her again in the church.

Questions

1. What does marriage mean to Marnie?
2. How long have she and Gary been together?
3. Did she ever love him?
4. How long has she been unhappy?
5. What does Gary look like?
6. What does Frank look like?

7. Marnie says Frank kisses "soft" whereas Gary kisses "hard." What's that mean?

8. Why did Marnie lie to herself and to Gary for so long?

9. What does she really want from a relationship?

10. What does she see in Frank?

11. What do her friends mean to her?

12. What does she do at the bakery?

13. Does she like her job?

14. What does the city mean to her?

15. Bock's language, punctuation, and phrasing are very specific. How do they help define Marnie?

Full Bloom
Suzanne Bradbeer

PHOEBE

I found this little, pottery-animal . . . thing I made when I was about . . . I don't know, six? It was in that box of stuff my Dad was looking through.

I can't figure out what it's supposed to be, a bear, or a . . . it's not a dog. It's not a definable creature, really. It's very sweet though, it has personality. And it's got this expression on its face . . . like it's trying to smile, but it's not smiling. Like it's anticipating something from you and has no idea what to expect. It's also got a very thick neck, but I don't think I did that on purpose.

Anyway, it's a very distinct creature, whatever it is. If I hadn't made it, and I saw it somewhere, at someone's house or somewhere, I'd think, "I'm going to like this person, whoever made this." At least, that's what I'd think if that person wasn't me.

Okay, I have a question.

If you give something to your Dad, if you give him something you made when you were six, something sweet, and distinct . . . don't you think he should take it with him when he goes?

Analysis: *Full Bloom*

Type: Dramatic
Synopsis

Suzanne Bradbeer's *Full Bloom* explores the fragile transition from childhood to adolescence. Phoebe Harris, a fifteen-year-old native New Yorker, is blossoming into a beautiful young woman. She is watching her parents' marriage deteriorate after her father left her mom for a younger woman. Meanwhile, her neighbor Crystal, a forty-something actress, is considering going under the knife because her career is suffering.

Youth and beauty are the recurring themes in Phoebe's life. She slowly begins to shrink under the pressure, acting in harmful ways that are out of character. She escapes to her balcony to look at the moon most every night. She skips school. She lies to her mother. She breaks dates with her father. She accepts a date with a popular boy at her school who once mocked her because of her looks. She avoids the advances of the handsome and charming young African American boy who has just moved onto her block and seems interested in her mind as well as her looks. Finally, she takes a paring knife to her face and makes a permanent scar.

Phoebe feels betrayed, not only by her father, but also by the world around her. Unfortunately, she isolates herself to such a degree that no one can get to her because she can't let anyone in. The play ends with an uneasy truce reached between Phoebe and her mother as they begin to step onto the road to healing.

Character Description
Phoebe, 15

Phoebe is named after the sister of Holden Caulfield in J. D. Salinger's 1951 novel *The Catcher in the Rye*. Phoebe is also the name of the goddess of the moon in classical mythology. These literary references enhance the kind of sensitive, educated environment in which Phoebe was raised. At the same time, Phoebe is not a spoiled or bratty child. She is privileged because of her multifaceted upbringing.

The play begins immediately following Phoebe's trip to Italy with her best friend. While there, she suffered a traumatic incident: a group of young Italian men surrounded her and, without touching her, led her into a deserted side street and admired her, leered at her. This violation of her personal space, this treating her like an object, has deeply upset Phoebe. This experience, together with her father's desertion of the family and Crystal's obsession with her looks, leaves Phoebe confused as to what really matters in the world.

Given Circumstances
Who are they? Phoebe is the main character.
Where are they? She is on her fire escape talking to the moon.
When does this take place? Contemporary.
Why are they there? She needs to get out of her apartment.
What is the pre-beat? Phoebe has just asked her friend Jim why he and his wife never had kids. He said they tried and couldn't but they had her, Phoebe, in their lives.

Questions

1. What is Phoebe's relationship to the moon?
2. Why does she no longer confide in her mother or Crystal?
3. Why does she no longer talk to her best friend?
4. Does Phoebe think her mother is beautiful?
5. Does she think Crystal is beautiful?
6. Why does this object hold so much importance to Phoebe?
7. Does Phoebe love her father?
8. How, specifically, does Phoebe feel betrayed by him?
9. How did Phoebe's experiences in Italy change her?
10. What does beauty mean to Phoebe?
11. What is life like growing up in New York City?
12. What is life in the apartment like without her father?
13. Why is Phoebe lying to everyone?
14. What does Phoebe think of boys her age?
15. What does Phoebe want from life?

All New People
Zach Braff

EMMA

Don't you believe in fate, Charlie? Here you are, in an empty beach house, on a deserted island, in the middle of the fucking winter, moments away from ending it all, when in I walk. Does that give you no pause? Maybe God sent me to provide you with some sort of . . . access to the doors of your mind that rusted closed. (Beat.) Sorry. I should tell you that I am super stoned right now. So if I say silly nonsense like that, you're gonna have to forgive me.

You want me to go. You've got things to do. . . Hmmm. You know you've put me into a smidgen of a moral conundrum here; you do realize that, Charlie. I don't think I can leave.

I think I may have been sent here to help. You may believe that or not, depending on where you stand on God and fate and destiny and all that; it's none of my business. But I do know that it's a little bizarre I walked in when I did, since I wasn't even gonna show them this house because it's outside their price range. This morning they called up and asked to see it. Out of the blue. Spooky. A religious person might think God intervened. I don't know what you believe but . . . Jesus or Moses or Mohammed, Vishnu, who's the one with the arms? The elephant with all the arms?

Ganesh. I doubt it was Ganesh; kind of simple assignment for a god with so many arms. But whomever your god is, I think may have channeled an intervention through two cranky old Jews from the Newark suburbs. I think I'm here to help. So why did you tie a noose around your neck, my new friend?

Analysis: *All New People*

Type: Comedic
Synopsis

Charlie has escaped to the summer vacation town of Long Beach Island, New Jersey, in the middle of winter. He knows the town will be deserted and he can be alone. As the play begins, he is contemplating hanging himself with an extension cord. He is interrupted when a young British real estate agent comes in to the show the house. From that point on, Charlie's pity party turns into an actual party as more unexpected strangers arrive and refuse to leave.

Zach Braff's dark comedy is unrelentingly ruthless and funny. More than creating a reflection on life and death, Braff is exploring the extreme lengths people go to in order to survive. Emma, the real estate agent, is here because she has recently had her rapist murdered in prison a few days before his release. Myron, a local firefighter, is desperately in love with Emma. He was formerly a drama teacher at the local high school but was let go for doing drugs and drinking with students at a cast party. Kim is a struggling singer who supports herself by being a professional escort. Charlie's friend Kevin owns the house in which the action takes place, and he has sent Kim to Charlie in an effort to cheer him up.

Late in the play, it is revealed that Charlie is an air traffic controller. He was distracted for a moment at work and two planes collided, resulting in the death of six people. It also happens to be Charlie's thirty-fifth birthday. He is at a crossroads.

Braff's play walks a fine line between realism and absurdism. It is anchored in reality by the very primal needs of its leading characters, but the almost ridiculous comic situations push it to another level. Ultimately, it is clear that these four characters need to come together. They are united in their hopes and their fears. They end up healing each other and finding some hope in their aimless lives.

Character Description
Emma, early to mid-20s
Born Clementine Thomas, she was nicknamed Emma by her mother, who died of breast cancer when Emma was eight. Emma's father is a bartender at a local pub.

A British citizen, Emma is trapped in the United States because she hired someone to murder her rapist in prison just days before his release. The killer has told Emma she cannot return to the country once he completes the act.

She needs to rent this house, any house, in order to keep her job and keep money coming in so that she can afford to live here while she figures out a long-term plan.

Myron is a good friend and desperately in love with Emma. She does not return the sentiment. He supplies her with high-quality drugs. She could marry him and stay in the States that way, but she considers it a last resort.

Emma is strong, tough, practical, and in control. She walks into a very high-stakes, and potentially dangerous, situation and manages to talk Charlie down (almost literally) from the ledge.

Given Circumstances

Who are they? Strangers who have just met.

Where are they? A summer home in New Jersey in the dead of winter.

When does this take place? Contemporary

Why are they there? Emma is a real estate agent there to show the house for rental.

What is the pre-beat? Emma has walked in on Charlie trying to hang himself.

Questions

1. Why is Emma stoned?
2. How stoned is she?
3. What's it like to walk into a house you think is empty, while stoned, to find a man trying to hang himself?
4. Does Emma believe in fate?
5. Does Emma believe in God?
6. How does she remain so cool under such high stakes?
7. Does she find Charlie attractive?
8. Why does she want to help him?

9. What does she think of this small New Jersey summer town?
10. How desperate is she to stay in America?
11. How did she get into real estate?
12. Does she like her job? If so, what does she like about it?
13. Does she miss home?
14. Why doesn't she marry Myron and solve her problem?
15. Does she regret having her rapist murdered?

Mercy
Laura Cahill

ISOBEL

Yeah, well, it is so over and I'm really happy about that. He is such an asshole even Sarah can tell you.

I'm so, so, so much better off without him I mean god, could you imagine? He's such an asshole. He doesn't really believe in anything which is why I guess he could never believe me. He never seemed to believe anything I said. Especially when I was trying to tell him how I felt. He would just look down and say, "You cannot feel that way," or he would laugh. He really would, he would laugh and I'd say, "Why are you laughing at my feelings? I mean everybody knows you're not supposed to do that and that someone's feelings are their feelings and they can't be right or wrong." There's no right or wrong feelings everyone knows that. And he'd say, "I have to laugh because you can't possibly feel that way," or "I don't understand." He'd say, "I don't understand," to like everything I would say. He wouldn't respond. There would never be any back and forth. And then last time I talked to him he started to cross the street! We were on 8th Avenue and he just started to cross the street while I was between two sentences. So I go with him across the street and he said, "I'm gonna go in there and get a bagel for the morning." So he got a couple of plain bagels in a little white bag and he was just holding it. All prepared. While I was feeling like . . . so I finished my sentence and then he got in a cab. He's awful. He's so awful. I'm so happy I'm not with him. He's . . . I don't know if there are words. I don't know if I could put it in a sentence, you know? How he is.

He's an asshole.

It's just that . . . I gotta wonder sometimes. It seems to get quieter when I'm talking. It's like as soon as I open my mouth—all of a sudden—I can only hear me. It can be kind of uncomfortable. And I want to know for real. You can tell me the truth. How can I do anything about it if I don't know? Right?

Am I boring?

Analysis: *Mercy*

Type: Seriocomic
Synopsis

In Laura Cahill's funny, touching, and unsettling play, everyone is talking but no one seems to be listening. At one point the character Sarah reads aloud from her journal: "General feeling of emptiness and loss. Sort of—almost. I have a feeling of almost." Whether written in this journal or spoken out loud, no one responds.

This feeling of "almost" pervades the entire play. Each of the four characters seems to be (or wants to be) on the brink of something, something indefinable, yet not a single one of them can commit to achieving it. If these young people could muster up the courage to actually <u>do</u> something, make a decision, take a step, put their feelings on the line, then life would perhaps take a turn in their favor. They are, however, frozen. They cannot find a "flow" in life because they are unable to see past themselves.

Isobel, the main character, is heartbroken over her recent breakup with Stu. Stu is a doctor who dreams of being a writer. Sarah, Isobel's best friend, says she wants to cheer Isobel up, but she spends most of her time aggressively pursuing Bo. Bo has recently declared himself a singer/songwriter after a failed attempt at acting.

These four people are unable to make any kind of meaningful connection with each other.

At the end of the play, Isobel declares her love for Stu. His response to this outpouring of emotion is, "I don't know how to respond to that." Therein lies the tension of the play: no one knows how to respond to each other's needs. Isobel, more than any of them at the moment, needs some mercy in her life, but no one around her can grant it.

Character Description
Isobel, early–mid 20s

Isobel is the main character of the play. Of the four characters, she's the only one who reaches any kind of self-awareness or emotional clarity. Whether her declaration of love to Stu is real or a moment of desperation, it is a huge accomplishment for her to reach out and make such an emotionally naked confession.

Cahill purposely provides little information about Isobel outside of her relationship with Stu. We know nothing of where she lives, where she grew up, what she studied in college, or what she does for a living. Isobel is someone who defines herself solely in regard to the man she is dating. The breakup has forced her into a tailspin.

When Stu appears at Sarah's apartment for dinner, Isobel goes from ignoring him, to passive aggression, to slipping back into her role as girlfriend, answering questions for Stu.

When Stu rejects her declaration of love, Isobel dissolves into tears. Then, just as quickly, she pulls herself together and goes out into the New York night with the group for gelato. Again, that feeling of "almost" pulses heavily under the surface. Isobel comes very close to achieving something but then settles for less than she deserves.

Given Circumstances

Who are they? Isobel and Sarah are best friends. Stu and Bo are friendly. As a group they are strangers and relate to each other as such.

Where are they? Sarah's Upper West Side apartment.

When does this take place? Contemporary.

Why are they there? A dinner party.

What is the pre-beat? Sarah and Bo have just been discussing what they would ask a psychic if they went to one, and now it's Isobel's turn.

Questions

1. How did Isobel and Stu meet?
2. How long had they been together?
3. Who and what precipitated the breakup?
4. What did Isobel find attractive about Stu?
5. Is she still in love with Stu?
6. What's the longest length of time Isobel has ever been single?
7. What does Isobel want to do with her life?
8. What is her relationship to Sarah?
9. Why are she and Sarah friends, and how long have they known each other?
10. What is her relationship to Bo?
11. Has she read Stu's book? What did she think of it?
12. Why did she not leave Sarah's apartment, knowing Stu was coming?
13. What is urgent about this monologue?
14. Why would she stay in a relationship for so long with someone who wouldn't listen to or accept her feelings?
15. What if she is actually boring?

Lascivious Something
Sheila Callaghan

DAPHNE

Do not be ridiculous. I commanded respect at that age. I had many friends, even the ugly girls. They threw a party for me at fifteen. It was a surprise. I remember I had stolen a dress that day. Did I tell you about this?

I stole a designer dress from the department store. I could have bought it myself. I had the money . . . it was a very pretty dress. It had sparkle, you know? Those bits that catch the light. Not diamonds, the other word. But I didn't want it badly enough to pay. And it was my birthday. I thought if I got caught I would tell the men it is my birthday, and they would let me take if anyway. But I did not get caught. In the room where you try things on, I put on the dress, then I put on my longer dress over it, and then I walked home. And my heart was so light. And I arrived home and my house was full of my friends, all smiling and eating little food on plates. And there was a pile of *cadeaux* in the corner, eh, gifts. And I took off my long dress and beneath I was sparkling, and everyone shouted "Ahhh!" and applauded. As if I could have known I had a party waiting for me. It was luck! I've always been lucky like that.

I could sparkle for you now, if you like. I will become a
holiday. I will decorate myself with twinkle lights and sing a
song about a man who buries his heart in the dirt and later
eats the dirt to remember how the heart tasted.

I will behave myself around your *amour perdu*.

Analysis: *Lascivious Something*

Type: Dramatic
Synopsis

Lascivious means "lewd" or "lustful." The "lascivious something"
that gives the play its title enters in the form of Liza, an American
woman in her late thirties, who arrives on a small Greek island in
search of her ex-boyfriend. August, also American and in his late
thirties, is there and now married to Daphne, a twenty-four-year-
old native to the island. August and Daphne live here, tending the
grape vineyards and making their own wine. Daphne is pregnant,
and they plan on staying here forever to raise their family. Liza
arrives on the day of the harvest and the day before August is to
taste the first batch of wine he's made.

The action of the play takes place in 1980 on the eve of famous former actor Ronald Reagan's election as president of
the United States. August and Liza, aside from being a couple,
were political activists together attempting to stop something
like this election from occurring. August left town when he realized he couldn't do it anymore. The violence and uneasiness
that follow in the next decade or so in America are mirrored
in the violence and uneasiness that shaped August and Liza's

relationship. Mirroring our country's desire for conspicuous consumption, Liza (allegedly) bit off a piece of August's skin near his hip after a sexual encounter. This threat of violence pulses through the spine of the entire play. As more secrets are revealed and the past becomes present, no one is innocent, and no one gets what he or she wants.

Callaghan, perhaps influenced by the classical roots of Greece, imbues the story with magical realism. Some scenes descend into chaos as that which should remain unspoken comes to the surface with primal force, only for the scene to restart itself and take a more civilized course.

Character Description
Daphne, 24

Callaghan describes Daphne as "poised, striking: a dark flower with a long, willowy stem." She is a native of this remote Greek island. She is no stranger to hard work. He family owns the land on which she and her husband, August, work. She is a few months pregnant. Daphne and August have been together for seven years. They met in America, where Daphne was spending her semester abroad. She was an art major and working on a photo essay of vineyards in Napa Valley. August was working as an apprentice at one of the vineyards she visited.

Daphne has been ostracized from her village. She has a weakness for beautiful things, including young girls. She had an intimate relationship with one and the town found out. August and Daphne have a one-person helper in the form of Boy, who is really a young girl.

The arrival of Liza throws Daphne's life into chaos. She hopes that one more violent sexual encounter between Liza and August will finally rid them of their desire for each other, but it does not.

Given Circumstances

Who are they? Daphne is talking to August, her husband.

Where are they? The porch of their home, under a trellis of grapes.

When does this take place? 1980.

Why are they there? They tend the vineyard and make wine there.

What is the pre-beat? August has invited Liza to stay for the wine tasting.

Questions

1. Is Daphne in love with August?
2. How threatened does she feel by Liza?
3. Does she think Liza is attractive?
4. Does she sense the chemistry between August and Liza?
5. How far along is Daphne in her pregnancy?
6. Does she like living on her home island?
7. Has she given up dreams of being an artist?
8. What is it she finds attractive about the young people she sleeps with?
9. Why does she return to the scene of her "crime"?
10. Does she have friends on this island anymore, other than August and Boy?

11. She knows August's first batch of wine is a failure; why doesn't she tell him?

12. Does she really want August to sleep with Liza?

13. Why doesn't she send Liza packing immediately?

14. What are Greek husband/wife relationships like?

15. What was life in the 1980s in America and abroad like: culturally, politically, and so on?

Almost, Maine
John Cariani

GLORY

Do you mind? Oh, no, I think you mind! No, you do! You *do*! Oh, I'm sorry! I didn't think you would! I didn't think—. You see, it says in your brochure that people from Maine wouldn't mind. It says (*Pulling out a brochure about Maine tourism.*) that people from Maine are different, that they live life "the way life *should* be," and that, "In the tradition of their brethren in rural northern climes, like Scandinavia," that they'll let people who are complete strangers, like cross-country skiers and bikers and hikers, camp out in their yard, if they need to, for nothing, they'll just let you.

I'm a hiker. Is it true? That they'll let you just stay in their yards if you need to? 'Cause I need to. Camp out. 'Cause I'm where I need to be. This is the farthest I've ever traveled—I'm from a part of the country that's closer to things—never been this far north before, or east, and did you know that Maine is the only state in the country that's attached to only one other state?!?

It is! Feels like the end of the world, and here I am at the end of the world, and I have nowhere to go, so I was counting on staying here, unless it's not true, I mean, is it true?

Would you let a hiker who was where she needed to be just camp out in your yard for free? I mean, if a person really needed to, reallyreally needed to?

Oh, I'm so glad, then!! Thank you!!

Analysis: *Almost, Maine*

Type: Comic
Synopsis

Almost, Maine is modern magical realism. In a series of unrelated scenes, each a meditation on love in one form or another, John Cariani creates a world in which anything is possible. The events of the play unfold over the course of one cold winter's night under the Northern Lights.

This particular monologue is from the scene titled "Her Heart." Glory has come to Maine seeking forgiveness from her recently deceased husband. She read somewhere that the Northern Lights are torches that the dead carry with them as they cross into the next world.

Glory has set up camp on a stranger's front yard because she read in a brochure that one could do so. Glory carries with her, in a paper bag, the literal pieces of her broken heart. The stranger named East, who owns the property on which she has camped, unexpectedly keeps kissing Glory. Each time he does so, he somehow winds up holding the pieces of Glory's broken heart. East is a repairman, and it soon becomes apparent that he not only fixes broken machinery, he fixes broken hearts as well.

Character Description
Glory, 20s

Glory is heartbroken, literally, and consumed by guilt. Her heart broke when her husband left her. It turned to slate and shattered into many pieces. The doctor replaced this broken heart with a new, artificial one. After the surgery, her husband came to visit her in the hospital and asked Glory to take him back. Unfortunately, she discovered that this new heart no longer desired him. Devastated by this news, Glory's husband ran out of the hospital and was hit and killed by an incoming ambulance.

There is an attractive innocence about Glory. She needs to believe that the Northern Lights are torches and that one belongs to her husband and she can find forgiveness. There is also something naive about someone who believes she can camp on a stranger's front lawn because a brochure said she could.

She is determined. She has a clear objective. She has more love in her than she is willing or ready to give at the moment.

Given Circumstances

Who are they? Glory and East are strangers to each other.
Where are they? East's front yard in Maine on a cold winter's night.
When does this take place? Contemporary.
Why are they there? Glory has set up camp in East's front yard.
What is the pre-beat? East has come out because he's seen Glory's tent pitched in his front yard.

Questions

1. Where has Glory come to Maine from? How long was the drive?
2. Why hasn't she traveled far in any direction before?
3. Why didn't Glory knock on East's door and introduce herself when she arrived?
4. Is Glory an outdoorsy person? Or did she purchase all this gear for this trip?
5. How long were she and her husband together?
6. Was her husband her first love?
7. Where did she come across the Maine brochure?
8. Has she always believed in an afterlife?
9. Does her new heart feel different from her old heart?
10. Why does she carry the pieces of the old heart in a paper bag?
11. What does she plan on doing with the pieces once she sees the Northern Lights?
12. Why does she need her dead husband's forgiveness?
13. What did her ex-husband look like?
14. What does East look like? How is he different from her ex?
15. How is Maine different from where Glory is from?

Snow Day
Eliza Clark

LINDSAY

I never see you anymore. What the fuck, Nate? I mean, seriously. You live one block from us and it's like you're a total stranger. Look at you. Are those pajamas? What kind of grown-up person are you?

I know Mom's not gonna volunteer to drive me to Steve's house. She thinks Steve cooks meth, even though I tried to explain to her that Steve couldn't cook a popover or like a Stoeffer's much less a ton of crystal methamphetamines, she's convinced he's a drug dealer. So I'm not allowed to go over there and you don't ever come over anymore, and now you're not even coming to Christmas, and it's been snowing for two goddamn weeks and suddenly the whole town is made of snowplows and salt, so we never get a minute off, and Bob and Mom are on me, like all the fucking time, about AP Euro and Vassar and being a contributing member of the household and making them proud, probably cause you're such a disappointment. I'm sorry. I don't mean it like that, 'cause you never disappointed me. Not once, Nate. Except now, when you won't ever come over and you don't even call me and you haven't responded to even one of my many desperate e-mails. You are the only

person in this town, in this whole world maybe, what do I
know, I only spend time in this stupid town, who makes any
sense and I wasn't sure you were coming to Christmas and
I wanted to spend an afternoon with you. So what's up? I
called in a bomb threat. Sue me.

Analysis: *Snow Day*

Type: Dramatic
Synopsis

It is two days before Christmas. Nate, late twenties, works in a
dingy, depressing thrift store. Lindsay, fifteen, is Nate's sister. She
comes in, in the middle of the day, because someone at school
phoned in a bomb threat and all the students were released after
questioning. It is snowing outside, and Lindsay keeps referring
to the early dismissal as a "snow day."

Lindsay wants Nate to drive her home, but he says he can't
leave the deserted store because his boss would get mad. Lindsay
goes around touching things, playing with the paging system,
criticizing the state all of the items are in. She wants to spend
time with Nate.

Nate left this small town two years ago to pursue life in New
York City. It didn't go exactly as he had planned. He's been working at the thrift store since returning, hardly talking to his family
and not talking at all to his friends. Carol, a police officer and former classmate of Nate's, comes in looking for Lindsay. It appears
she's a suspect in the bomb threat. Nate lies and says Lindsay's
not there while catching up with Carol.

It seems like things aren't going well for him here, either. Carol is married to the former football star. Nate is a failure. He doesn't even have plans to spend Christmas with his mother, sister, and new stepfather. He wants to be alone.

Both Nate and Lindsay are having "meltdowns." Lindsay did, in fact, call in the bomb threat. After Carol leaves, Nate promises he'll sneak Lindsay out somehow and that they can spend some time together.

Character Description
Lindsay, 15

Lindsay is having a hard time. Her mother and stepfather are pressuring her about grades, college plans, and the future. Her bother, Nate, whom she greatly admires, has been back in town for two years but lying low, unseen, in the dingy thrift store.

Lindsay phoned in the bomb threat because she wanted a snow day. She was bored and wanted something exciting to happen. She feels as if no one listens to her. Now she regrets it and feels badly.

This monologue succeeds in getting Nate to protect her. Instead of driving her home, Lindsay asks if they can just sit on the dirty old couch and stay there together for a while. And they do.

From Up Here
Liz Flahive

LAUREN

Are you going to the dance? Do you have a date? Why don't you ask my brother to go?

I mean, as his official ambassador, don't you think it's your responsibility? To help him have a good time? Seriously? That's strange because you ask everyone questions about him, you stare at him all the time. And now you're over at our house. It looks like you really want on him.

Why do you need to know everything about him? Really. And you're not writing all this shit about my brother for your college essay? And you're going to lie about it to my face?

Bullshit. I heard this teacher talking about how she was so moved by what you wrote about "the Barrett boy." They're going to publish it in all the papers. Apparently it's very well written. Lots of detail. Mrs. Gordon said it gets inside his head, makes you realize just how disturbed he must have been. How teachers still can't get other kids to sit near him in class. You know how that medicine gave him that tic under his left eye and if he can't get it under control he gets so upset his hands start shaking.

She wrote about that because the school nurse fucking
TOLD HER and . . . I told him not to talk to anyone.
Why does everyone need to know about that? Why do
you have to write about my brother? Why don't you write
about something else?

Analysis: *From Up Here*

Type: Dramatic
Synopsis

Kenny Barrett, a high school senior, has threatened his high
school with an act of unspecified violence. The act was unsuccessful, but the resulting aftershocks are deep and lasting. He has
been allowed back into school, but under the provision that he
be constantly supervised, on campus and at home. The potential
of the event has left everyone in Kenny's family feeling unsettled.
This unsettled feeling mixed with a sharp dose of violence causes
the play to practically vibrate.

Grace, Kenny's mother, and Daniel, her new, much younger,
husband, are on uncertain footing. Daniel is keen on starting a
new family, bringing a new child into their lives, while Grace
feels she can't handle the children she has now. The household
is thrown into further chaos by the unexpected arrival of Caroline,
Grace's unpredictable younger sister. Kenny feels an affinity for
Caroline that he does not share with his mother. This relationship further pushes Grace off balance.

Kenny's younger sister, Lauren, is confused by the actions of
her brother. She's trying desperately to understand why he was

planning the attack, why he would hurt himself and others, and why he would leave her alone. She is surprised and confused by the sudden attention of Charlie, an upperclassman. Charlie doesn't look at her strangely, or as the sister of a freak. He simply sees her.

From Up Here is about holding on to each other even when the world seems to be falling apart around you.

Character Description
Lauren, 15–16

A seemingly typical high school sophomore, Lauren plans her clothing rotation a week in advance. When the play opens, she is searching for clothes that were to have been picked up from the dry cleaners by her brother, Kenny. He forgot. Typical.

Lauren is dealing with her mother's new marriage to a younger man on top of her brother's actions. He is now a social outcast at school, and this greatly affects the status of an underclassman. At the same time, she loves her brother dearly and goes to great lengths to protect and defend him.

Lauren is initially mistrustful of Charlie's advances. Lauren knows what people are saying about her, and she finds it difficult to believe that anyone can truly be interested in her simply for who she is, on the inside and the outside. Although defensive with Charlie on the outside, she slowly begins to let him in and get to know her.

The school has assigned Kenny a mentor, Kate, who follows him most everywhere, even home after school. When Lauren discovers the real motivations behind Kate's actions, she confronts her in this monologue.

Given Circumstances

Who are they? Kate has been keeping an eye on Kenny at school. Lauren is Kenny's sister. Grace and Kenny are also present.

Where are they? The kitchen of Lauren's home.

When does this take place? Contemporary.

Why are they there? Kate is helping Kenny prepare his speech to the school.

What is the pre-beat? Lauren has just entered and been introduced to Kate.

Questions

1. How does Lauren feel about her brother's potential act of violence?
2. How does she feel about her mother's new husband?
3. How does she feel about the reputation she's garnered at school for being "easy"?
4. Why is she so protective of Kenny?
5. How is she dealing with the fact that suddenly everyone is paying attention to her?
6. What does "family" mean to Lauren?
7. Why does she confront Kate in front of Kenny and Grace?
8. What does Lauren want from Kate?
9. Lauren is going to the dance with Charlie. How does she feel about that?
10. Has she ever had a boyfriend before?
11. What does Charlie look like?
12. How does Charlie make her feel?
13. What kind of student is Lauren?

14. How big is their school?
15. What is urgent about this monologue?

Milk Like Sugar
Kirsten Greenidge

ANNIE

College expensive. I read and shit, but my marks and stuff ain't so good for that. These teachers are chumps. We got the same books my mom had here.

Books're tricky . . . tricky things. Used to keep mine in the kitchen. "I know this one," my mom says one time. Got all excited. Went through all the pages. Got all—. Probably couldn't barely read it back in the day, and she sure as hell can't really now—. I stood there listening, her fingers tracin' over the type. Her voice searching. Don't leave no books out no more. Made me feel—. She looked up once she realize she could barely read it, her eyes nearly—. Her lookin' at me like that I felt my whole chest just sitting there open, like she could see something in me don't smell right to her. Couldn't tell what—. . . . She stood there. Stood there. Then she shut the book quick. She much always got house stuff for me to do after that. She think it time for homework, all sudden it time for pine-sol. Shoot. That better than seeing her with that book. Try not to bring up nothing like that ever now. I hear her talk about that stuff and I can't even—.

I'm, I'm tryin' to find a more excellent way.

Analysis: *Milk Like Sugar*

Type: Dramatic
Synopsis

It is Annie Desmond's sixteenth birthday. She is celebrating with her best friends, Margie and Talisha, by going to a tattoo parlor. Annie initially wants a ladybug, but under pressure from Talisha, who says that is silly and childish, she decides on a small red flame on her hip. This pull between childhood and maturity is the main theme of the play. The three girls also form a pact on this day, sparked by Margie's pregnancy, to have babies at the same time.

Milk Like Sugar paints a startlingly candid take on the adolescence of African American inner-city youth in contemporary America. Annie's home life is difficult. Her undereducated mother, Myrna, is a cleaning woman who dreams of being a writer. Her father is mostly absent. Her friends care more about which boy has the best new cell phone and what kind of designer baby gear they'll get than anything else. Talisha is in a relationship with a much older man who abuses her. Margie's man is mostly undefined. For these girls, the joy of having a baby comes from the need for unconditional love. They feel unloved, unwanted, unseen by most everyone in their lives.

Annie, a sophomore, begins a relationship with Malik, a senior. Her friends encouraged this relationship because of his new red Slidebar phone that is "almost as nice as those Blackberry ones." Their first encounter is awkward. Annie, so intent on sleeping with him to get pregnant, can't see that he is interested in more than sex with her. Malik wants to get to know Annie.

A young girl named Keera, a transfer student, enters the play and brings with her a world of hope for Annie. She has a close, happy home life. They have a game night. Keera has a strong relationship with God. The combination of Keera and Malik's influence guides Annie toward making more positive, proactive choices in her life. Unfortunately, when Annie discovers Keera's life is a lie, she acts out by sleeping with her tattoo artist and subsequently finds herself pregnant from the encounter. One bad choice derails the rest of her life.

Character Description
Annie, 16
Urban, African American young girl struggling with the onslaught of adolescence and peer pressure. Annie is close to her friends and victim of their opinions. She begins a relationship with Malik because of the kind of phone he has. Her eyes are opened when she discovers that he wants more from life than the hand he's been dealt and is working hard to get out of the life he currently lives.

Annie is hurt, frustrated, and disappointed in the failure she perceives her mother's life to be. Fortunately, Malik and Keera give her a fresh perspective on the world. She begins to make better decisions because of them.

Given Circumstances
Who are they? Annie and Malik.
Where are they? The clearing in the park.
When does this take place? Contemporary.
Why are they there? It is their second date.

What is the pre-beat? Annie has just looked through a telescope for the first time, and Malik has just kissed her.

Questions

1. What does Annie dream of doing with her life?
2. How is she defined by her urban surroundings?
3. How does she use language and what does it say about her?
4. What does being a mother mean to her?
5. What does she like about Malik?
6. What does he look like?
7. What does she want from him?
8. How does she see the world on a daily basis?
9. How does she see the world differently from this clearing?
10. Why does her mother's lack of education bother Annie so much?
11. What did she see when she looked through the telescope?
12. What did the kiss make her feel like?
13. How is she different with Malik than she is with her friends and family?
14. Does she want to go to college?
15. What does she think her flame tattoo says about her?

Bachelorette
Leslye Headland

GENA

Speaking of which . . . blowjobs are a delicate thing, my friend. You can't just go all out at the beginning of the relationship or affair or whatever. You gotta savor it which makes them savor it. You gotta make them feel like you're holding something back. You know?

Look. On a scale of one to ten, one being, like, you blow it kisses and ten being you're choking on vomit and semen. You gotta start out with fours and fives. You're just good enough that they feel like you know what you're doing but you're aloof . . . right? No enthusiasm. So he'll think, "Fine. I'll just fuck her." You start off with a ten and you've got nowhere to go. Why is he gonna spend any time fucking you when he just came all over your face? But if you start small . . . Then you build up to it. Give him a six after a fight. Give an eight when he spends a lot of money on you.

Eight is like . . . in the car. While he's driving. On the way to your parents' house for Christmas.

Then you go back to fours and fives when you want him to do something like propose.

And his dick alarm will go off. And he'll be like, "What's wrong, baby?" when really he means, "Suck my dick harder."

Analysis: *Bachelorette*

Type: Comedic
Synopsis

Leslye Headland's dark comedy explores the tensions, jealousies, and petty rivalries that exist among four female friends. All of these feelings are especially heightened by the fact that Becky, the overweight and least popular friend, is getting married the next day to a rich, successful, handsome man. Her three "friends" deal with their jealousy by escaping into a night of alcohol, drugs, and sex.

Becky has asked Regan to be a bridesmaid even though the two are no longer close. She has even asked Regan to spend the night in her bridal suite on the condition that Regan not invite Katie and Gena. Regan, of course, does just this.

Regan is a perfectionist and the queen bee of the group. Seemingly perfect on the outside, she is dependent on numerous prescription medications. Three years into a long-term relationship, Regan can't understand why she's not the first to get married. Gena is the sexiest of the group and, in many ways, the most mature. She is struggling to recover from a recent breakup. Katie is the true beauty of the three. She is utterly lost. Still working retail since graduation, she seems to have no real goal in life. She has no relationship. She regularly drinks to the point of blacking out. On this particular evening, she mixes the booze with marijuana and cocaine in an almost deadly combination.

All three of these girls are searching for love but are unable to accept when a man is truly interested in them. This fact is illustrated by the interactions we see between them and Jeff and

Joe, two men they pick up and bring back to the hotel. Both are nice guys, but nice guys finish last with these ladies.

Becky has learned to be mean from these girls. She has learned to manipulate. The deterioration of the evening culminates in a standoff between Becky and Regan that is simultaneously chilling and heartbreaking. These girls are not, and have never been, friends.

Character Description
Gena, early 20s

Gena (pronounced "Jeh-nuh") is a "force to be reckoned with." She is the most compassionate member of the group, and also the most in control.

Gena understands that she and Becky are no longer friends, so she is troubled by the fact the three of them have been invited to celebrate. She doesn't know that Regan has been asked specifically not to invite them along.

Gena is still hurting from her breakup with Clyde. The breakup also coincided with an abortion, a fact that Regan casually drops in conversation to hurt Gena.

However, as this monologue proves, Gena belongs in this group of women if solely for her powers of manipulation. This piece proves she is just as skilled at passive-aggressive behavior as the rest of them. Underneath the surface, though, she cares for her friends. She is the only one able to care for Katie when she blacks out late in the play.

Given Circumstances

Who are they? Best friends.

Where are they? An expensive New York City hotel suite.

When does this take place? Contemporary.

Why are they there? The night before their less popular friend's wedding.

What is the pre-beat? Regan wants to know why her boyfriend hasn't proposed yet.

Questions

1. How long have these young women been friends?
2. What keeps them together?
3. What do they like about each other?
4. What does Gena like about herself?
5. What does she specifically not like about herself?
6. Why does she self-medicate, excessively, with drugs and alcohol?
7. What is Gena's level of self-awareness?
8. Why does Gena show up tonight knowing Becky doesn't want her there?
9. What does Gena really think of Becky?
10. Why did her relationship with Clyde end?
11. How long were they together?
12. Does she regret the breakup? The abortion?
13. Why are these girls so passive-aggressive?
14. What is Gena afraid of?
15. What does Gena want from a relationship?

4000 MILES
Amy Herzog

BEC

Sometimes right-handed people sit at the left-handed desks and I get really pissed. Yeah. I'm like, you're not hurting me, you're hurting yourself.

I don't want to talk about college with you, Leo. Because you're just gonna be, like, disdainful.

It's . . . I don't know, everyone's so much younger than me, I mean just two years, but it seems like . . . so it's lonely. But I'm taking this class on global health that I think is really . . . I met with the professor a couple times and I might help her with some research next summer in Mumbai, if the money works out.

I walked into her office and I was like, I've built houses in Ecuador and taught English in Mali and installed solar panels in Kathmandu and I want to know how I can work with you. And she was like, "Wow, it's so refreshing to meet a female undergraduate who doesn't end every sentence in a question mark." So . . .

It'll be nice to travel somewhere not on my parents' dime, you know?

I want to break up. The other night when I said I needed some time to think, that wasn't true, I want to break up.

Analysis: *4000 Miles*

Type: Seriocomic

Synopsis

Twenty-one-year-old Leo is on a cross-country bike ride from Seattle to New York with his best friend, Micah, when tragedy strikes. Micah dies in a freak accident and Leo continues on the journey, alone, until he winds up on the doorstep of his ninety-one-year-old grandmother, Vera. Leo has no cell phone or computer on his trip, and his family and loved ones are worried over not hearing from him as well as surprised and disappointed that he doesn't return for Micah's funeral.

Leo and Vera strike up an unlikely, mutually beneficial friendship for the few weeks that he lives with her, each providing the other with much-needed companionship. Leo has a girlfriend, Bec, and they are on uncertain ground. It is revealed that under the influence of peyote, both Leo and Bec made out with Leo's adopted sister, Lily, over the summer, throwing his parents and Lily into a tizzy.

Leo finally finds a job in Colorado and decides to move there after making a short visit back to Seattle to try to smooth things over. The play ends with Leo practicing a short speech he's written about his grandmother's next-door neighbor and closest friend who dies.

Character Description

Bec, 21

Bec is strong, beautiful, and a good foil for Leo. She is hurt and disappointed by Leo's refusal to fly home for Micah's funeral. She is also upset that Leo showed up on her doorstep unexpectedly a few nights ago. Bec has come to Vera's apartment to talk with Leo, who is late, leaving her to sit and have coffee with Vera.

Bec is athletic, which Vera constantly misinterprets as fat. Bec is unforgiving, as witnessed by her very strong reaction to Vera's story about her continually adulterous first husband. Bec has, in fact, been planning on breaking up with Leo for some time—even before the trip. She canceled her plan to join Leo and Micah on the ride cross country, perhaps because of this. She is driven and confused by Leo's lack of ambition. And she feels as if Leo is constantly disappointed in her. She is both furious at and worried about Leo.

Given Circumstances

Who are they? Longtime friends and lovers.

Where are they? Vera's Greenwich Village apartment.

When does this take place? Contemporary.

Why are they there? Leo has asked Bec over. She is there to end their relationship.

What is the atmosphere? Tense. They had a fight the last time they saw each other.

What is the pre-beat? Leo was late, leaving Bec alone with Vera and running late for class. He has just asked her if they have left-handed desks in college.

Questions

1. How long were Bec and Leo a couple?
2. How did they meet?

3. When and why did Bec begin to think she wanted to break up?

4. Why did Bec not talk to Leo when he first showed up at her door a few nights ago?

5. Why did Bec take time off before going to college?

6. What did she learn about herself and the world from her trips overseas?

7. Was she with Leo when she made these trips? How did that affect them?

8. Why did she come to see Leo on an afternoon when she has class?

9. Why does Vera's story about forgiving her cheating husband upset Bec so much?

10. Does she still love Leo?

11. How close was she to Micah?

12. What was the funeral like?

13. How difficult was the funeral without Leo?

14. How difficult was it not being able to talk to Leo about the accident?

15. What are some of the things she has done/not done that Leo finds disappointing?

Speech and Debate
Stephen Karam

DIWATA

Sometimes, when all the stalls are taken in the girls' room at school, I use the boys' bathroom on the third floor, because no one is ever up there after three. And I shout first, I say, "Anyone in there?" you know, something like that.

So last year when we were rehearsing for *The Crucible*, there was a line of girls, we were all in costume waiting to use the bathroom . . . so I went up to the third floor, and I yelled into the boys' room. No one answered, so I went in. I finished going to the bathroom, and I heard footsteps. Normally, I'd rattle around, make noise pulling toilet paper out, you know, trying to let someone know I'm there, I'm a master at masking the sound of plopping poop. But because this is the guys' bathroom . . . I was just kind of holding my breath, thinking I'll wait it out. And then more footsteps. Maybe they came in together, I can't remember . . . but I could see them through the crack in the side of the door. Mr. Healy for sure, and then him, with those white sneakers. Their backs were to me.

He never looked at Mr. Healy, both of them seemed to be pee-ing, but then Solomon seemed to be standing further away from the urinal, like he was . . . I dunno . . . like he was trying to show Mr. Healy his . . . you know? And there was some touching, I don't remember exactly how it started, because then I breathed, I inhaled, they must have heard; they didn't check to see who was in the stall, they just bolted, both of them.

And that was it. I sat in there for about twenty minutes. I was scared. *I* was scared, isn't that weird?

Analysis: *Speech and Debate*

Type: Seriocomic
Synopsis

Three high school students with little in common are brought to-gether in an unlikely friendship because of a sex scandal. Stephen Karam's funny and incisive play explores how the internet brings some people together while, simultaneously, ripping others' lives apart. Diwata, Howie, and Solomon are the ultimate outcasts in every way, but they find power and comfort in each other.

Diwata, seventeen years old, wants the leading role in all of her high school productions. She never gets them and details her trials and tribulations in an online video blog. In an attempt to campaign for the role of Lady Larkin in the upcoming production of *Once Upon a Mattress*, Diwata implores people to email the drama teacher, Mr. Healy, and posts his email address. Howie, eighteen, recognizes the email address as belonging to someone who propositioned him for sex in an online chat room. Howie contacts Diwata by leaving a message on her page, and it is seen by Solomon, sixteen, an aspiring reporter.

Diwata, desperate to perform, takes control of the school's Speech and Debate Team, but she needs at least three members for it to be recognized. She bribes, blackmails, and schemes the boys until they relent. Howie and Solomon need information in order to get to the bottom of the scandal, but more than that, they need friends. Things between the three friends get tense as a series of revelations come out and they learn more about each other. Everyone has secrets in this world, and they're pretty serious.

Karam's play explores the power of technology for good and bad. It also highlights the importance of theater and dance, not only for building community, but also for creating a political platform. The three teens present a hilarious and touching performance piece that aims to find the common humanity in us all. In the end, the three outcasts are united by a common cause that provides them with hope, friendship, and confidence.

Character Description
Diwata, 17
Diwata is smart, annoying, pushy, challenging, and driven. She never stops to feel badly about herself, because she's always thinking of the next way to get ahead. Although she bribes and blackmails Howie and Solomon into being on the team, she does so without a hint of evil and malice. She wants a place to belong and people to be there with her.

When not recording her video blog or working on her musical adaptation of Arthur Miller's *The Crucible*, Diwata is a waitress at the local diner.

Diwata has recently had an abortion. She tries to keep it a secret, but Howie spied her going to the clinic. Her sexual partner goes unnamed and mostly unmentioned. The sexual experience, as described, appears to have been unsatisfying and incomplete.

Diwata pushes her boundaries and works outside of her comfort zone. She covers her vulnerability through an outgoing facade. As she is seemingly fearless on the outside, her admission of fear in this monologue is a huge revelation.

Given Circumstances

Who are they? Students at the same high school who hardly know each other.

Where are they? The diner where Diwata works; Salem, Oregon.

When does this take place? Contemporary.

Why are they there? Diwata wants Howie to join the Speech and Debate team.

What is the pre-beat? Howie has some information for Diwata that he's reluctant to share.

Questions

1. What aspect of performing does Diwata enjoy most?
2. Who are her friends?
3. What is her daily routine at school like?
4. Whom does she talk to?
5. Does she get good grades?
6. Why does she keep a video blog?
7. Why does Arthur Miller's play *The Crucible* mean so much to her?
8. How did she meet this boy she had sex with?
9. Why did she have sex with him?

10. Was she scared to get an abortion?
11. What does the Speech and Debate club represent to her?
12. Does she enjoy waiting tables?
13. Diwata refers to herself as "not perfectly pretty." How does she feel about that?
14. What keeps her fighting after so many rejections?
15. What is urgent about this monologue?

Well
Lisa Kron

LISA

Okay, so every year I would get invited to Susie's Halloween party. And every year I would think about my costume, believing, as I did, because my mother told me that it was so, that there was nothing more important or valuable than originality and creativity.

And the first year I went to the party, after a great deal of thought, I decided I would go as the Little Match Girl — which doesn't sound all that original I know, but I decided to do it *authentic*.

And so I found these nasty clothes in the basement somewhere and ratted my hair really bad, and there was dirt, like, I rubbed real dirt all over myself. And the result was, I have to say, excellent. And I could not wait to get to this party and walk in and be like: "This is it, girls, this is what real creativity looks like."

And I got to this party and I walked in, and I saw that all the other little girls, every one, was dressed as a beautiful princess. And I thought: Okay. This is not going to work out the way I pictured it. You're all princesses and I'm clever, sort of, but not really, because I'm covered in dirt.

And then we spent the rest of the day playing this game called "Fairies," which is a game in which you go outside and run around the perimeter of the yard pretending to be a fairy. And the fun of this game, if you happen to be dressed as a princess, is you feel the breeze blowing through your pretty hair and you can feel your pretty dress fluttering behind you and you feel really pretty. That's the point. And I played along because—what else was I going to do? I had actually chosen ugliness. For some reason I couldn't remember anymore, I had actually chosen ugliness and now I had to clomp around in it surrounded by fluttering beauties. I thought to myself—and not for the first time—Adulthood must surely be better than this. And I vowed the next year I would also be a princess.

Analysis: *Well*

Type: Comedic
Synopsis

Lisa Kron is a solo performance artist who, in this play, invites other actors onto the stage with her as well as her mother, Ann. Lisa guides the audience through her carefully structured "exploration" of themes dealing with sickness and health. Alternating between scenes from Lisa's childhood in Lansing, Michigan, when Ann served as president of the neighborhood association, spearheading the integration movement there, as well as Lisa's time as a teenager in a Chicago hospital's allergy unit, Lisa is attempting to understand why some people are sick while others are healthy.

By placing her mother on stage with her, Lisa has committed the ultimate act of self-sabotage. Ann constantly derails Lisa's stories, challenges Lisa's depictions of past events, befriends the other actors in the play, and, finally, propels Lisa to sit at the top of the stairs, pouting. Ultimately, Lisa has to come to terms with the fact that this play is about her anger at the sickness that slowed her mother down for most of her life. She learns that integration means "weaving into the whole even the parts that are uncomfortable or don't seem to fit."

NOTE: Although *Well* may be the most unconventional play in this compilation in terms of form and structure, it is still a satisfying and complete theatrical event. Lisa, although based on the actual writer Lisa Kron, is still a character in this play and should be approached as such.

Character Description

Lisa, any age

Lisa is a solo performance artist. In this particular play she has introduced a group of other actors onto the stage with her, including her mother. At the same time, she stubbornly insists that this play is not about her relationship with her mother.

Lisa suffered from an illness so strong as a young woman that she had to go to an allergy clinic in Chicago for testing. She was sick like her mom was sick. What she found was she actually got better when she moved away from home, not through any major discoveries while in the unit.

Lisa is a careful planner. She wants to the audience to see the past through her rose-colored glasses, not necessarily the way they really were. Aside from her mother constantly interrupting her, a little African American girl who bullied Lisa as a child keeps storming onto the stage and mocking Lisa.

While Lisa loves her mother dearly, she is angry with her for being sick and, as Lisa sees it, not doing anything to make herself well.

Given Circumstances

Who are they? Lisa is an actor, talking to the audience. She is on stage with her mother.

Where are they? In a theater, with Lisa's Lansing, Michigan, home recreated on the stage.

When does this take place? Contemporary.

Why are they there? Lisa is exploring the concept of what makes us some people sick and some people well.

What is the pre-beat? The other actors have lost track of what the next scene is, and Ann has asked Lisa to tell the following story.

Questions

1. Why has Lisa invited her mother on stage with her for this show?
2. How did Lisa's childhood illness affect her sense of self?
3. How does Ann's illness affect the way Lisa lives her life now?
4. Has Lisa ever in her life felt like a fairy or a princess?
5. Aside from making her mother happy, what does Lisa learn from telling this story?
6. Why does Lisa remember this story so vividly?

7. Does Lisa still feel like the Little Match Girl to this day, out of place, out of sync?

8. Where does Lisa's sense of individuality come from? Her mother?

9. How does Lisa think she and her mother are alike? Different?

10. How often do Lisa and her mother talk when they're not in the same city? Daily? Weekly?

11. What kind of things does Lisa keep secret from her mother?

12. What aspects of her life does Lisa share with her mother?

13. Is Lisa afraid of turning into her mother?

14. Why does Lisa put her personal life on display for an audience?

15. Is Lisa well? If so, how? If not, how so?

Brooklyn Boy
Donald Margulies

ALISON

No offense or anything, but fiction is like *so* over.

I mean, don't get me wrong, I *love* books. And I really respect people like you who still bother to write them. Like watchmakers or violin-makers or something. People who devote themselves so completely to a dying craft? It's touching, it really is. I don't know how you do it. I really don't. It takes a lot of courage to do what you do. Who do you do it for? I mean, besides yourself. Who's your audience? Middle-aged or old people who have the time and the money to buy books and read them? That's nothing; that's like a tiny, miniscule fraction of the population. Kids *my* age don't read. They don't. I mean, it's not that they're illiterate, it's just that it's not an important part of their lives. The only stories *they* like are the kind that can be *shown* to them. All they have to do is sit there and let it wash over them. I mean, why read when they could much more easily go to a movie or rent a DVD or something? Why spend like thirty bucks on a book that might not even be any good 'cause even books that are *supposed* to be good are rarely as good as they say they are, they're just hyped up to get you to buy them.

I'm sorry. I'm not saying this is how *I* feel, I'm saying this
is how kids my *age* feel. I wanted to meet you. You know
how you read a book and you want to meet the author? If
you *do* meet them . . . you pray to God they don't turn out
to be a schmuck or something? You're doing okay. I liked
your voice when you read tonight, at Book Soup.

Analysis: *Brooklyn Boy*

Type: Seriocomic
Synopsis

Eric Weiss is a novelist in his mid-forties. Jewish, born and
raised in the Sheepshead Bay area of Brooklyn, Eric has spent a
lifetime either dodging or running away from his roots. Donald
Margulies's play is about accepting all of the aspects of our life
that combine to make us who we are, even the uncomfortable
ones. We can't pick and choose what made us, but we can accept
and learn from it.

Brooklyn Boy is the title of Eric's third, and his most commer-
cially successful, novel. Walking a fine line between fiction and
memoir, it is a thinly veiled account of Eric's childhood growing
up in Brooklyn and the people around him. Eric's first two novels,
The Gentleman Farmer and *The Aerie*, were critical successes but
perhaps a bit too esoteric for mass consumption. Eric's friends
and relatives complain that they didn't understand what those
two books were about. *Brooklyn Boy*, however, is just about to
reach number 11 on the *New York Times* bestsellers list, and Eric
is launching on a national book tour.

Eric's professional life is taking off while his personal life is falling apart. He is in love with his wife, but they are getting a divorce. His father, Manny, lies dying in a Brooklyn hospital. Manny seems to be either constantly criticizing his son or not taking a vested interest in him or his work. The novel forces Eric to come to terms with his entire life.

While in Los Angeles to work out the details of the screenplays for *Brooklyn Boy*, which sold for millions of dollars, Eric picks up a young woman at a book reading. He's living a life he's never dreamed of: rich, successful, suddenly attractive to younger women, and housed at the fancy Mondrian Hotel. Alison represents the kind of girl he never had access to in the past.

Eric finally comes to terms with everything when Manny, after dying, appears to him telling him he loves the book and that Eric got everything right. Eric realizes that who he was and who he is aren't all that different.

Character Description
Alison, early to mid-20s
A Los Angeles girl through and through, whether born there or a transplant. She sees life in terms of status, fame, and success. Although she purports to read novels, her own writing is for the cinema. She has written a science-fiction screenplay about a utopian society on the brink of ecological disaster. The youth try to overthrow the leaders, who happen to be their parents, with destructive results. The point of the screenplay is that the children are as clueless as the parents (notice the parallels in theme here).

Alison read *Brooklyn Boy* and wanted to meet Eric. She liked the sound of his voice at the reading. She's also read his other two novels. Although she claims she is not a "literary groupie," she is in Eric's hotel room at two in the morning to sleep with him. Eric refuses and sends her back in a cab.

Given Circumstances

Who are they? Eric, a famous writer, and Alison, a fan.

Where are they? Eric's fancy hotel room in Los Angeles.

When does this take place? Contemporary.

Why are they there? Eric has invited Alison back after she introduced herself at his reading.

What is the pre-beat? Alison has just explained her screenplay to Eric, and he asked what makes it a movie and not a book.

Questions

1. If Alison thinks fiction is over, why has she read all of Eric's books?
2. What were her expectations going into the book reading?
3. Is she attracted to Eric?
4. What does he look like?
5. Does she plan on sleeping with him? Why?
6. Eric is much older than Alison; what does she think of that?
7. Has she ever been in such a fancy hotel room?
8. What drives Alison to write?
9. What is her next project?
10. How much has she written in her life?
11. Where is she from originally?

12. What brought her to Los Angeles, and how long has she been there?

13. How much education has she had?

14. How/why does she think she's different than other kids her age?

15. What is the objective of this monologue?

Victoria Martin: Math Team Queen
Kathryn Walat

VICTORIA

I'm *popular*. Like totally, undisputedly popular. Like, I walk down the hallways, and even though I'm a sophomore, there are seniors—senior *guys*, with deep voices—who say: *Hey.* Sometimes they say: *Hey, Vickie, what's up?* Like, they know my name.

OK, so mostly they're on the basketball team so they know my boyfriend, who is totally varsity first string, even though he's only a junior, because this fall while the other guys were playing football all he did was practice his free throws, because he's a one sport guy. Scott. He's totally into me. And that's why I'm a *sophomore* and those senior jocks know my *name*, but it's not like I'm one of those slutty girls whose name all the guys know, and plus I totally have girl friends too.

I'm friends with the *Jens*. Who are on the varsity cheerleading squad, even though they're sophomores, mostly because all the juniors who tried out this year had "weight issues" so forget trying to get *them* up in a pyramid—plus, the Jens are very, very peppy. They know how to do that thing where they toss their ponytails, and depending on the toss, it's either like: What*ever*, I am so walking away from *you*. Or, it's like: See this swish? That's right, this ponytail says: I will see *you* later.

I understand this distinction. I am not a cheerleader. But I *know* this. I have secured my place in the high school universe, after the very volatile freshman year, which the Jens and I refer to as: Versailles. Like, the Treaty of Versailles? You know—World War I, European power struggle, third-period history with Mr. Delano—that's where we met, our desks, in a row, across the back of the room: Jen—Me—Jen.

Yesterday, at the math meet? All of that was suddenly meaningless. This one kid had an equation on his T-shirt. The quadratic formula across his back. I *know*! I mean, nerd central, *all* math geeks, *and* I was the only girl. Except for these two on the other team, who would only speak to each other. In binary. For fun. And when I was in the girls' bathroom and I totally just got my period, and had to ask one of them for a pad, they just *giggled*. And so I had to stuff all of this scratchy school-grade toilet paper into my underwear and meanwhile, I almost missed the sophomore round of questions, because they put all the room numbers in Roman numerals. For fun. And when I finally got there, I was sitting next to this kid who kept clicking his retainer and it was driving me crazy, and I was like: I don't *do* headgear, OK?

Analysis: *Victoria Martin: Math Team Queen*

Type: Comedic
Synopsis

Victoria Martin is a popular high school sophomore. Her two best friends—the Jens—are varsity cheerleaders. Her boyfriend, Scott Sumner, is a junior and the varsity first string on the basketball team.

The Math Team is suffering debilitating losses after its star player, Sanjay Patel, moved to Arizona. At the prodding of her math teacher, Mr. Riley, Victoria secretly shows up to a Math Team meeting. She loves numbers. She's good with them. Victoria's parents are in the middle of a divorce, and her father has moved across the country, to California. A love of math and numbers is something she shares with her dad. Being on the Math Team is a way for Victoria to stay close to him.

However, being on the Math Team also puts Victoria's popularity at great risk. The Jens would never understand. She would be labeled a geek. She creates a series of lies and evasions to explain her sudden change in schedule to the Jens and to Scott. The consequences extend beyond this. Victoria finds herself kissing Peter, a fellow team member, on the night of Scott's big game, and word quickly spreads when Jimmy, a freshman with a huge crush on Victoria, sees the kiss and reports it immediately.

Victoria Martin: Math Team Queen is a touching, funny, and honest look at the roles we're assigned in high school, sometimes outside of our control, and how we can maneuver them to our advantage or even redefine ourselves.

Victoria discovers that the personal happiness and rewards she finds as a member of the Math Team outweigh those of just being popular.

Character Description
Victoria, 16

When we first meet Victoria, she is very comfortable in her popularity and the self-created drama that goes with it. She has power in being a sophomore with a junior boyfriend who is a varsity sports star. She has power in being best friends with the two Jens. None of this power means anything to Victoria, however. She is shattered by the divorce of her parents and feels lost with her father living so far away. Obsessed with Pi, Victoria spends her time memorizing the sequence of numbers, hoping one day that there will be an end to it.

She unexpectedly finds peace in joining the Math Team, even if it means lying to her "best friends" and her boyfriend. Victoria learns that popularity does not necessarily equal happiness but that being true to herself does.

As the only girl on the team, she also inadvertently teaches the boys on the team a few lessons in gender relations, etiquette, and self-awareness.

Given Circumstances

Who are they? Victoria is talking to the audience. (You, the actor, need to make this more specific.)

Where are they? Victoria's bedroom.

When does this take place? Contemporary.

Why are they there? Victoria is on the brink of a crisis.

What is the pre-beat? Victoria enjoys being on the Math Team even though she's risking her popularity.

Questions

1. What does "popular" mean to Victoria?
2. Is she in love with Scott, or attracted to his popularity?
3. What does she like about the Jens other than their popularity?
4. How has her parents' divorce affected Victoria?
5. Why does Victoria join the Math Team?
6. Is she willing to risk her popularity and commit to the team?
7. What's the difference between a freshman, a sophomore, a junior, and a senior?
8. Why was her freshman year so volatile?
9. How does she know so much about European history? Does she enjoy it?
10. How does a math meet work?
11. How does Victoria relate to her teammates on the otherwise all-boy team?
12. Who are her friends other than the Jens?
13. Whom does she tell really personal stuff to?
14. What is it about numbers and math that makes her feel so safe/good?
15. How difficult are things now that her father lives across the country from her?

ACKNOWLEDGMENTS

This book would not have happened were it not for the kindness and generosity of my friend and colleague Bruce Miller.

I also must thank the University of Miami class of 2014 for their talent, time, and input. They gladly offered up class as well as personal time so that I could hear these monologues out loud: Amandina Altomare, Brandon Beaver, Javier DelRiego, Kristin Devine, Marilyn Hadsell, Annette Hammond, Mikhail Hellerbach, Adam Maggio, Mona Pirnot, Clare Rea, Alanna Saunders, and Maggie Weston. They taught me as much as, if not more than, I taught them.

A huge amount of gratitude must be extended to Marybeth Keating of Hal Leonard for her patience, guidance, and support.

To all my teachers and mentors—there are almost too many to name—who had a hand in shaping my view on theater and how I teach it: Helen White, Jim Carnahan, Nicky Martin, Rob Marshall, Sam Mendes, John Crowley, David Leveaux, Susan Bristow, and Amy Saltz.

To the people who read and advised initial drafts of the book: Katya Campbell, Heather Diack, David A. Miller, and Saidah Arrika Ekulona.

To all the playwrights and agents represented here for their permission.

To Joe Ferrari for never-ending love, support, and patience.

Finally, to my mother and father, who always supported this path.

PLAY SOURCES AND ACKNOWLEDGMENTS